Seven Wonders of the New World

A Captivating Guide to the Great Wall of China, Colosseum, Petra, Christ the Redeemer, Machu Picchu, Taj Mahal, and Chichén Itzá

Free Bonus from Captivating History (Available for a Limited time)

Hi History Lovers!

Now you have a chance to join our exclusive history list so you can get your first history ebook for free as well as discounts and a potential to get more history books for free! Simply visit the link below to join.

Captivatinghistory.com/ebook

Also, make sure to follow us on Facebook, Twitter and Youtube by searching for Captivating History.

Table of Contents

INTRODUCTION 1

CHAPTER 1 - THE ORIGINS AND HISTORY OF THE GREAT WALL
OF CHINA 3

CHAPTER 2 - THE LEGEND OF MENG JIANGNÜ: THE WOMAN
WHO TORE DOWN THE GREAT WALL.................................11

CHAPTER 3 - THE COLOSSEUM: ROME'S MOST POPULAR
WONDER IN ITS GLORY DAYS 18

CHAPTER 4 - FROM SAND TO SEA: GLADIATORIAL COMBAT
AND NAVAL REENACTMENTS AT THE COLOSSEUM 27

CHAPTER 5 - PETRA: A WONDER WITH MYSTERIOUS
BEGINNINGS 35

CHAPTER 6 - PETRA: THE ENVY OF THE ANCIENT WORLD'S
SUPERPOWERS 43

CHAPTER 7 - THE ARRIVAL OF THE PORTUGUESE ALONG THE
SHORES OF BRAZIL 50

CHAPTER 8 - CHRIST THE REDEEMER: BRAZIL'S SYMBOL OF
FAITH 56

CHAPTER 9 - THE CONQUEST OF THE INCA: TRIUMPHS AND
TRAGEDIES 62

CHAPTER 10 - THE MISIDENTIFICATION OF MACHU PICCHU 69

CHAPTER 11 - SHAH JAHAN, THE RISE OF THE MAN WHO BUILT
THE TAJ MAHAL..78

CHAPTER 12 - THE TAJ MAHAL: A SYMBOL OF LOVE BEYOND
MEASURE..84

CHAPTER 13 - THE REDISCOVERY OF CHICHÉN ITZÁ 94

CHAPTER 14 - THE COLLAPSE OF THE MAYA CIVILIZATION AND ITS WONDROUS CITIES 104

CONCLUSION 111

HERE'S ANOTHER BOOK BY CAPTIVATING HISTORY THAT YOU MIGHT LIKE 114

FREE BONUS FROM CAPTIVATING HISTORY (AVAILABLE FOR A LIMITED TIME) 115

BIBLIOGRAPHY 116

Introduction

It was sometime in 450 BCE, and Egypt had just welcomed a special guest. His name was Herodotus, and he hailed from the lands of the Olympian gods: Greece. The man was humble, but he was not merely a traveler. He was a scholar and historian who craved to see the world beyond his borders.

Upon arriving in the lands of the pharaoh, Herodotus was struck with awe the moment he saw the kingdom's architectural splendor. The Greek historian not only recorded wars and political conflicts in his book but was also on the hunt for the world's best sights and structures. And so, upon setting eyes on the Great Pyramids, Herodotus quickly put the descriptions of the colossal structures into words, hoping to share his journey with the world.

The pyramid was not the only structure Herodotus had jotted down in his ancient record. He spent most of his life traveling from one region to another; thus, it is safe to assume his records were filled with descriptions of dozens of impressive architectural wonders he stumbled upon. Perhaps satisfied with the number of wonders he had scribbled down in his journal, Herodotus thought it was time to compile them into one. And so, he journeyed back to the Library of Alexandria, where he would spend hours reading scrolls and writing his latest work.

With the help of Callimachus of Cyrene, Herodotus came up with a list of world wonders that compiled a set of architectural marvels all over the world he had set foot before. The list probably functioned like modern-day travel guides that suggest wondrous destinations to tourists.

Herodotus' list of wonders may have given detailed insight into each magnificent structure and the history behind its construction. Sadly, the list is forever lost to us, as it had long succumbed to the challenging test of time.

Fortunately, a handful of writers during the Middle Ages preserved fragments of his accounts. Through their efforts, we have been granted a precious opportunity to delve into the wonders of antiquity. However, imagination is all we can rely on today; just as his list, all the wonders that impressed Herodotus centuries ago have long vanished, ravaged by wars, natural disasters, or simply the passage of time. Only one endured—the Pyramid of Giza—giving us a small glimpse into the thriving ancient world.

Nevertheless, humanity's unyielding spirit has continually pushed the boundaries of possibility, resulting in the construction of new wonders that captivate our imaginations. Through the ages, new marvels have been brought forth, each with distinctive features and remarkable tales. From an engineering triumph that spans thousands of kilometers of rugged mountains and valleys to a colossal amphitheater and an all-marble mausoleum, these new wonders stand as evidence of the indomitable human spirit and the unrelenting pursuit of greatness. In this context, Herodotus' list found new life; from the Wonders of the Ancient World came a new list called the Seven Wonders of the New World.

Chapter 1 - The Origins and History of the Great Wall of China

Dragons were thought to be mythical creatures that symbolized evil—at least according to most old European beliefs. Though depicted with four legs and a long tail, these dragons also had a pair of large wings that could lift their enormous bodies off the ground, allowing them to travel across the vast skies. They guarded the world's most precious treasures and breathed fire to destroy those who dared to stand in their way—or, perhaps, tried to steal valuables. These fearsome creatures were often categorized as antagonists. The Chinese, however, had a completely different view, believing dragons to be far from malevolent creatures. They were, in fact, symbols of prosperity, good fortune, strength, and protection. Some even claimed they were rulers of the deep sea.

A depiction of a dragon carved onto a tomb.
BabelStone, CC BY-SA 3.0 <https://creativecommons.org/licenses/by-sa/3.0>, via Wikimedia Commons: https://commons.wikimedia.org/wiki/File:Coffin_board_with_dragon_engraving.jpg

Spotting the many differences between the two types of dragons is not a demanding task. Chinese dragons, or "loong," have a pair of horns on top of their heads. Apart from their visible sharp teeth, they also wear beards and whiskers. They do not have wings, but like their Western counterparts, they can fly. Their most prominent characteristic is none other than their body shape: Chinese dragons have a rather long, serpentine body fully covered in scales that are believed to glimmer under the sun, giving them an almost divine appearance.

Depictions of the serpent-like dragon no doubt appear on numerous ancient Chinese artifacts, arts, and literature. However, few know that the Great Wall of China was also a tribute to the mysterious creature. The wall that goes through the natural contours of the landscape is said to resemble the long body of the serpentine dragon sleeping across the land. Whether the legendary wall was intentionally designed to resemble the dragon remains a topic of dispute. However, we can be sure that just as dragons were important in Chinese myths and beliefs, the Great Wall also played a pivotal role in the ancient history of China. This giant structure was an impressive engineering feat that protected the kingdom from dozens of impending dangers for centuries.

Although the Great Wall of China is regarded as one of the wonders of the new world, its construction began many centuries ago—its history goes back to before China was reunited by its very first emperor. Much to the surprise of many, the Great Wall was initially not a single set of walls; instead, it began with a series of walls constructed during China's Warring States period.

Like the ancient Egyptians, Greeks, and even the Japanese, the Chinese went through a long period of divided kingdoms. Believed to have begun in 475 BCE, the Warring States period was when the different states of ancient China fought against one another, each vying for control, territory, and resources. Great battles, strategic alliances, and vicious betrayals were common during this point of time. New military tactics and defense strategies were continuously developed throughout these years.

Parts of the Great Wall originating from the Ming Dynasty.

The ancient Chinese were always renowned for their exceptional skills in building fortified walls. With the growing turmoil at the time of the divided kingdoms, having their territories heavily protected by defensive walls was deemed crucial, especially for the most notable contenders of the war: the states of Qin, Zhao, Wei, Yan, and Ming. These walls were used to defend themselves from each other and hold off any attacks by the nomadic raiders of the north.

The Great Walls of the Warring States

The state of Wei began as a small entity in the seventh century, but it grew tremendously over the centuries through strategic alliances and military conquests. By 403 BCE, Wei had become one of the leading states during the Warring States period. Though Wei often faced threats imposed by the nomadic tribes of the north, the state was also plagued by frequent conflicts with its neighboring state, Qin. And so, to resist attacks and protect its people from the powerful Qin, Wei began constructing its own fortified walls in 358 BCE. Made out of rammed earth and further reinforced by wooden beams, stones, and bricks, the Great Wall of Wei stretched along the Yellow River for over three hundred kilometers, bordering its greatest nemesis, the Qin state, on the west. Though the climate was harsh and the terrains were rough—the steep mountains had claimed the lives of many laborers—the construction was completed in just seven years.

Garrisons were placed along the wall, and watchtowers were installed to spot enemies from a distance. Despite successfully repelling daring enemies who wished to lay it waste, Wei eventually suffered a terrible loss when the forces of Qin rose to their ultimate power.

The state of Yan also had its own sets of walls to barricade its people from the dangers of the war. However, the construction of the walls was only launched after the state's successful campaign against the Donghu people. Under the reign of King Zhao of Yan, the formidable general Qin Kai is said to have defeated the nomadic tribe, clearing the way for the state to conquer the Liaodong Peninsula. Beginning at the recently-conquered Liaodong Peninsula, the Great Wall of Yan stretched into Chifeng and ran through the northern region of Hebei. Parts of the southern walls were then further fortified as a defense against the state of Zhao—which, like the rest of the warring states, had also secured its territories by erecting a series of fortified walls.

The most impressive of all was, of course, the walls constructed by Qin. Once a peripheral state with little influence in the Chinese political sphere, Qin transformed when reforms were introduced by a man named Shang Yang, who became the state's chief advisor. Through his reforms, the state's government was successfully centralized, and its military forces grew into a formidable power. Yang led his soldiers against the Wei and drove them out of the comfort of their fortified city. Years later, the Qin also obliterated the state of Yiqu (located northwest of Qin), leaving it with no choice but to submit. This, however, was only the beginning of Qin's aggressive expansion. In 221 BCE, under the reign of King Zheng, the Warring States period finally ended when Qin came out on top after having conquered the rest of the individual states.

Emperor Qin Shi Huang and His Great Wall: The Precursor to the Current Great Wall of China

King Zheng, later known as Qin Shi Huang (or Shi Huangdi) was the first emperor of unified China and the founder of the Qin dynasty. Historians, however, have mixed views of the autocratic emperor. Some considered him a hero for ending the centuries-long war and uniting China, while others claim he was an absolute brutal ruler whose obsessions were only power and immortality. (He was the famed emperor who launched several quests in search of immortality and was interred with thousands of Terracotta Army when he finally met his end.) Nevertheless, Qin Shi Huang was also the emperor who gave birth to the foundation of the Great Wall of China, which greatly protected the kingdom from harm.

Although the kingdom's east and west were protected by natural barriers—the Pacific Ocean and the Tibetan Plateau, respectively—its northern territories were exposed, making them highly vulnerable to the barbaric nomads who had long attempted to invade the Chinese lands and secure its agricultural wealth. And so, when the emperor noticed the increasing power of the nomadic Xiongnu, he dispatched 300,000 of his army against them without hesitation. Under the command of Meng Tian, the Qin army successfully drove the Xiongnu further northward, thus reversing their ambitious expansion plans. Not risking any more invasions from the north, the emperor laid out his grand plans to construct a single set of fortified walls known as the "Wan-Li Chang Cheng" or the "10,000-li Long Wall." Spearheaded by Meng Tian, the construction began, which connected some of the walls left by the former warring states.

Given how tremendous the project was, an unimaginable number of laborers were needed. Soldiers and commoners were enlisted to work on the walls. Hundreds of thousands of peasants and sentenced criminals were also conscripted to ensure the project's completion. Once chosen to lend their hands on the walls, the majority were not allowed to deny the work; they were guaranteed a sword to their necks should they defy their emperor. The construction was harsh, as the laborers were said to have been forced to work on the rammed earth and rocks collected from the mountainous ranges with only a short amount of rest. Many perished with tools still held firmly in their hands due to the merciless climate, exhaustion, and extreme dehydration. The bodies of the poor builders were either interred within the walls or in grave pits nearby. Despite the brutal construction process, the emperor's defense system was realized; upon completion, the wall spanned from Lintao in the west and into Liaodong in the east.

The fall of the Qin dynasty resulted in the disrepair of the wall, but the Han dynasty rulers soon restored it. The walls were repaired to their most glorious state, expanded, and greatly fortified with more watch towers. Under the Han, the Great Wall reached nearly 6,000 kilometers, covering the regions of Dunhuang to the Bohai Sea. The construction work on the walls during this period was no different than during the Qin dynasty; under the reign of Emperor Han-Wudi, forced labor continued, and the wall's reputation as the worst place of suffering spread beyond the empire's frontiers.

However, given the extreme length of the walls, the Chinese emperors were often plagued with a headache: constantly maintaining such a monumental structure would be unimaginably costly. Thus, the Great Wall fell into disrepair once again. However, in the 1200s, one particular force would recognize the wall's disuse as an opportunity to exploit it to their advantage.

At first, China flourished under the glorious reign of the Song dynasty. Scholars today often admire the Song economic revolution, as this was the period when China's agriculture, ironworking, and printing technologies grew tremendously. The dynasty also saw growth in the state's population, allowing the cities to thrive and transform into hubs of various activities. Unfortunately, as prosperous as the dynasty was, it was also forced to deal with the growing danger posed by its northern rivals: the ferocious Mongol warriors under the legendary reign of Genghis Khan. Under Khan, the Mongols formed a well-organized and exceptionally formidable army capable of overthrowing any forces— including the Chinese empire.

In 1211, the Mongols rode to the Juyongguan Pass and breached the Great Wall, destroying its reputation as the world's most impregnable fortification. Bribing the Chinese officials and guards, the cunning forces of Genghis Khan managed to penetrate the walls several more times until they eventually besieged the capital of Yanjing (known today as Beijing) in 1215. Though the city was plundered heavily, the Mongols never intended to sack it entirely. It was only in 1279 that the Mongols, under the leadership of Kublai Khan (the grandson of Genghis), successfully overthrew the Song dynasty. With their grand victory, Kublai Khan established the Yuan dynasty, which ruled over China for a century.

Under the Yuan dynasty, China faced no resistance from the north, which led the Great Wall into further disrepair. The structure was only refortified when the Chinese regained control over their empire. In 1368, the Mongols were defeated, and China was finally under the control of local emperors from the Ming dynasty. Learning from their past mistakes, the emperors reinforced the Great Wall using sturdier materials, such as modern bricks, stones, and mortar.

Watchtowers were also erected every three to five hundred meters along the walls—when enemies were spotted, guards on the watchtowers would signal for reinforcements using smoke, gunpowder, and flags. Towering over seven meters high with an impressive width of five to seven meters, the Ming Great Wall could accommodate either ten armed soldiers standing shoulder-to-shoulder or five cavalrymen in formation side-by-side. Along the walls, one could spot two types of openings: smaller ones created especially for the archers and bigger holes used to drop heavy rocks on advancing invaders.

View of the Great Wall from a watchtower.

The refortification project spanned a century and undoubtedly required immense labor and resources. Though much of the Great Wall succumbed to the test of time, many of its sections still stand tall today. In fact, it is the Ming Great Wall we often see as a backdrop for tourists visiting China.

However, the walls did not protect China for long, as the Chinese were, yet again, left with no choice but to bow down to the power they intended to repel. Noticing the chaos brewing in the capital of Beijing, the Manchurians quickly took action. They successfully overthrew the Ming and established the Qing dynasty, which later incorporated the Mongols. Under the Qing, China's territory expanded far into Mongolia and beyond the Great Wall. And so, the walls fell into disuse once again, and the structure eroded over time. The sturdy bricks and stones were plundered and used as building materials for other constructions. Nevertheless, parts of the walls served as a defense system one last time during World War II when the Chinese faced a possible invasion from the Japanese.

The Great Wall of China in 1907.
https://commons.wikimedia.org/wiki/File:Greatwall_large.jpg

Today, the fate of the Great Wall is somewhat ironic. Once built to keep invaders out of China, it now welcomes thousands of foreign visitors every year. While the original purpose of the Great Wall may be long gone, mentions of the structure will never disappear from our history books. The Great Wall of China has survived countless centuries of war, natural disasters, and neglect, yet parts of it still stand strong, providing us with a vivid image of the remarkable achievements of ancient China.

Chapter 2 - The Legend of Meng Jiangnü: The Woman Who Tore Down the Great Wall

The myth of Meng Jiangnü occurred sometime between 221 and 206 BCE when the Chinese kingdom was under the control of the emperor Qin Shi Huang. At the time, agriculture was the mainstay of the economy and the foundation of society. While the nobles and aristocrats enjoyed a privileged lifestyle flooded with abundant wealth, power, and prestige, the commoners belonged at the bottom of the hierarchy and order. Indeed, those at the top of the social pyramid had dwellings within the fortified city, each adorned with fine arts, sculptures, and furniture. However, the same could not be said of the less fortunate ones that made up the majority of the kingdom's population. These people could not afford to enjoy a life behind the safe walls of big cities, so they built their houses on the outskirts, with farming as their main source of income.

Far to the southern part of the kingdom lived a couple who went by the surname of Meng. They led nothing but a simple life. They would rise when the sun emerged on the horizon, and probably well-rested from their sleep the night before, the couple would begin working on their farm. Though their routine was the same every day, the Mengs found great joy and satisfaction in their work, taking pride in the small victories of each harvest and the humble pleasures of their lives.

One morning, as the Mengs tended to their farm, they found a small packet of bottle gourd seeds. Without expecting anything peculiar to happen, they planted the seeds in the rich soil of their yard. As the days passed, the bottle gourd vines grew with surprising vigor, twining their way around the walls of the Mengs' humble dwelling and creeping into the yard of their neighbors, the Jiangs. At first, the Mengs worried that the vines might be seen as an unwelcome intrusion. But to their surprise, the old couple welcomed them with open arms, eagerly tending to the growing crop alongside the Mengs. Thus began a warm and enduring friendship between the two families, marked by the simple pleasures of tending the vine and the shared joys of their daily lives.

As the days grew shorter and the leaves turned golden, the plant finally bore fruit and was ready to be harvested. Eagerly, the two couples gathered around the plant, marveling at the size and shape of the gourd that hung from its vines. With great care, they plucked it from the vine. Since they both took care of the plant equally, they decided to cut the gourd in half and share it with each other. To their surprise, what they found inside was like nothing they had ever seen.

A tiny, innocent infant lay curled within the gourd. The Meng and Jiang families watched as the infant opened her eyes as if she had just awakened from a deep slumber. It was indeed a peculiar event, but the two couples had no time to ponder about logic; instead, they were thinking of who would raise the child. Since both couples had no children, the two families decided to adopt the infant and raise her as their daughter. Combining their surnames, they named the girl Meng Jiangnü—a name that would soon echo throughout the kingdom.

Despite their modest lives, the two families blessed Meng Jiangnü with the most tender love and boundless care. Though they achieved only small victories from their harvests each season, the Mengs and Jiangs never failed to feed their beloved daughter to the fullest and made her contentment their top priority. In gratitude for their absolute care, Meng Jiangnü assisted with the household chores—she did so willingly and without a single complaint crossing her mind. Days turned into years, and Meng Jiangnü soon turned into a young, beautiful woman whose remarkable character and admirable qualities won the hearts of many.

Meng Jiangnü was said to have loved spending her leisure time strolling around gardens and parks, marveling at mother nature's beauty.

On one fine evening, as she was walking through a tranquil garden, Meng Jiangnü was startled by sudden rustling sounds from nearby bushes. Curious, she slowly approached the bushes to investigate the sound. Halfway towards where the bushes were, Meng Jiangnü froze the moment she saw a figure of a man hiding among the bushes—who, at the same time, was peering at her every move. Frightened, Meng Jiangnü began running away, with other sources claiming she went to fetch her parents.

Perhaps feeling guilty of unintentionally scaring her, the man quickly emerged from hiding while calling out to the fleeing Meng Jiangnü, asking her to stop. Dressed in tattered clothes, with a rugged look on his bare face, the man introduced himself as Fan Xiliang and reassured her that he meant no harm. Despite her initial fright, Meng Jiangnü noticed the sense of desperation in Fan Xiliang's shaky voice. And so, she decided to lend her ears to the mysterious man.

In an anxious tone, Fan Xiliang told Meng Jiangnü the real reason behind his hiding: he did not do so to stalk her but to avoid getting caught by the government officials actively conscripting men to work on the Great Wall. He added that he had been on the run for days and had not touched a single meal since leaving home. As Fan Xiliang explained his backstory, Meng Jiangnü grew to sympathize with his situation. She had also noticed something else as she listened to his story: beneath his desperate and rugged look, Fan Xiliang was a handsome young man whose gentle manner would attract anyone.

Without hesitation, Meng Jiangnü knew she must help Fan Xiliang. And so, she took the young man home and introduced him to her parents. Just over a short period, Meng Jiangnü and Fan Xiliang bonded as if they had known each other for years. They talked until they forgot the existence of time and laughed at each other's jokes until their worries disappeared—at least for a little while. Eventually, the two fell deeply in love and could not see a future without one another.

The story of Meng Jiangnü and Fan Xiliang's marriage has been told and retold in various versions throughout history. One version suggests Meng Jiangnü first expressed her desire to marry Fan Xiliang. She had seen his charming qualities and how gentle he was with her, and she immediately told her parents of her wish. Seeing how happy their daughter was with Fan Xiliang, the Mengs and the Jiangs agreed to marry them off without hesitation.

However, another source provides a slightly different perspective. According to this version, Fan Xiliang initially rejected Meng Jiangnü's marriage proposal. He was worried that she could be pulled into his troubles should she become his wife. Despite Xiliang's reservations, Meng Jiangnü was persistent and firmly stated that she would marry no one except him. Her unwavering love and determination eventually won him over; Fan Xiliang, who deep down could not bear losing her, agreed to marry her.

The two were married in a simple yet heartfelt celebration, perhaps with only a modest feast accompanied by a small group of close friends and neighbors. Despite their humble circumstances, their love for each other was strong, and they were filled with hope and optimism for their future. However, the world was not filled with only rainbows and sunshine. Unbeknownst to the newlyweds, their time together was shortened from forever to only three days.

An envious stranger had just learned the story of Fan Xiliang's initial hiding. Though details about the stranger are minimal, old writings suggest he had been in love with Meng Jiangnü. Though the love was only one-sided, he could not bear seeing her with another man. And so, out of jealousy, the man reported Fan Xiliang's whereabouts to the government officials.

As soon as the authorities received word, they wasted no time tracking down Fan Xiliang. Despite his clear protests and the pleas of Meng Jiangnü, who begged the officials for mercy, Fan Xiliang was dragged away and immediately taken to the construction site of the Great Wall. He had to leave behind the life he had dreamed of with Meng Jiangnü and accept a fate that many dreaded: to work day and night without rest on the wall until the construction was completed or he breathed his last breath.

The news of Fan Xiliang's arrest and forced labor on the Great Wall spread quickly throughout the small village, leaving Meng Jiangnü devastated and beyond heartbroken. She had just begun building a life, but without Fan Xiliang by her side, their home felt empty and devoid of warmth. Instead of spending her free time wandering around gardens and surrounding herself with nature, Meng Jiangnü stayed indoors. She spent endless hours gazing at the stars, praying for a miracle, and hoping for a way to reunite with her beloved husband.

A year passed, and Meng Jiangnü never heard anything from her husband. She was constantly plagued with nightmares each night, with the recurring dream of Fan Xiliang dressed in thin clothing, shivering terribly as he moved one brick after another in the heavy winter snow. Longing for her husband and worried about his state on the construction site, Meng Jiangnü grew determined to find a way to hold Fan Xiliang in her arms again. And so, her routine changed one day: she began filling her autumn hours with knitting clothes, each padded with cotton to keep her husband warm. Knitting kept her occupied all day and eventually filled her eyes with the hope of finally reuniting with Fan Xiliang again.

Nevertheless, Meng Jiangnü knew that finding her husband at the Great Wall was no easy task. She had heard rumors of the harsh conditions and the many deaths during the wall's construction. But the rumors did not stop her from continuing her mission. She asked around and gathered information on how to reach the site. Finally, she set off on a long and treacherous journey, traveling only by foot and relying on the kindness of strangers to get her closer to her destination—and, soon, closer to the gentle touch of her dear husband.

After months, she finally arrived at the foot of the Great Wall, which lay on the present Shanhaiguan Pass. There, Meng Jiangnü was met with the sight of endless lines of workers exposed to the harsh temperature of winter, each carrying heavy bricks to arrange on the Great Wall. With haste, Meng Jiangnü searched among the workers, calling out Fan Xiliang's name over and over again. Her voice echoed through the walls, but there was no answer, let alone a response from a voice she longed for. Her voice grew hoarse as she desperately called out her husband's name.

Meng Jiangnü only stopped calling when she noticed a man approaching her. Also a forced laborer, the man claimed to have known her husband. Unfortunately, the next few words that came out of his mouth broke Meng Jiangnü's heart into a thousand pieces. He informed her that Fan Xiliang had died some time ago, and his body had been interred within the walls like hundreds of others who succumbed to the same end. Noticing that Meng Jiangnü had turned frozen from the news, the man offered to lead her toward the spot where her husband had been buried.

Only after arriving at the section of the wall where Fan Xiliang had been interred and left to rot was Meng Jiangnü able to express her feelings. She wept continuously, and some claim her tears fell down her cheeks non-stop for three consecutive nights. On her last day of weeping, the sky turned black, and a fierce wind began to blow, though no rain ever touched the ground. Instead, her weeping had invited chaos; in the blink of an eye, a section of the wall that measured at least four hundred kilometers long crumbled to the earth's surface, exposing many human remains buried under the wall.

Nevertheless, Meng Jiangnü could not identify Fan Xiliang's remains. And so, she prayed to the gods for a way to recognize her husband one last time. She then bit her finger until her blood ran down her arm. She let a drop of her blood touch each corpse and skeleton on the ground along the ruins of the wall. It was said that the blood would only dissolve when it touched Fan Xiliang's remains, and that was how Meng Jiangnü finally identified her husband. The moment she saw the blood dissolve, her heart was filled with relief and sorrow. Indeed, she had found her husband, but he was gone forever.

An illustration of Meng Jiangnü weeping by the Great Wall.
https://commons.wikimedia.org/wiki/File:Meng_Jiang_Nu_Song_Dynasty_Lie_Nu_Zhuan.jpg

The story of Meng Jiangnü did not end there. At the time of her arrival at the construction site, Emperor Qin Shi Huang was also nearby to tour the progress of the Great Wall. And so, when a section of the wall collapsed, word traveled fast enough that the emperor managed to confront Meng Jiangnü before she could depart with her husband's remains. The emperor was popular for his cruelty; thus, it was no surprise when he immediately punished the person responsible for the collapse.

However, upon laying eyes on the devastated young woman, the emperor immediately grew fond of Meng Jiangnü and wished to marry her. Meng Jiangnü knew defying the emperor would never end well, so she had no choice but to agree. But she had no plans on making the marriage easy. She proposed three conditions to the emperor before they could wed. First, her deceased husband must be given not only a proper funeral but also a grand one. Second, the Chinese court, including the emperor himself, must mourn Fan Xiliang's terrible fate. Third and last, Meng Jiangnü wished to visit the sea.

Of course, the emperor was not entirely happy when Meng Jiangnü requested to honor her dead husband; after all, he was but a commoner whose name he did not know. But he was headstrong on marrying her, so the emperor agreed to all three conditions.

When the funeral was done, and Fan Xiliang's remains were finally put to rest, Meng Jiangnü moved on to her next plan. No force on earth could make her marry the man responsible for her husband's demise. And so, when the emperor fulfilled her third condition, Meng Jiangnü jumped into the Bohai Sea, drowning herself, hoping she would be reunited with Fan Xiliang in another life.

The legend of Meng Jiangnü is a powerful reminder of the harsh reality faced by countless peasants who worked on the construction of the Great Wall. Although the tale blurs the lines between fact and fiction, it is rooted in historical truth. The legend offers a vivid glimpse into the struggle of those who worked tirelessly to build one of the world's greatest wonders and serves as a reminder that behind every great work of history lies a complex and often tragic human story.

Chapter 3 - The Colosseum: Rome's Most Popular Wonder in Its Glory Days

It was the 18th of July in 64 CE, and the Romans were about to welcome a tragedy into their city unwillingly. The first few signs could be seen in the merchant shops close to the Circus Maximus, Rome's famed chariot-racing stadium. Huge clouds of smoke began to form in the air, followed by screams of terror echoing from one corner to the other. Soon, high winds came, spreading terror to the northern districts. The citizens' slumber was disrupted, and they all burst through their doors, hoping to escape from death and catch a whiff of fresh air once again. Many, however, failed, falling lifeless on the ground with their flesh burnt to a crisp. Houses became ashes in a split second, Romans resorted to looting and violence, parents lost their children, and the poor lost faith in living. While hundreds were engulfed in the blazing fire, those given mercy by the angry ancient gods were spared, though they had nothing left. They were left homeless, without a coin in their coffers. This was one of Rome's greatest tragedies—a merciless incident that took the life of many and destroyed over half of the Eternal City. This was the Great Fire of Rome.

A depiction of the Great Fire of Rome.
https://commons.wikimedia.org/wiki/File:Robert,_Hubert_-_Incendie_%C3%A0_Rome_-.jpg

Where was Nero, the reigning emperor, when the great chaos took over his city? the Romans might have angrily wondered. Some said he was aware of the fire devouring his city but had made himself comfortable and was playing music behind the safe walls of his villa far from Rome. Others claimed he was the one who instigated the fire. Whether these accusations should be considered remains a dispute. However, none could deny that his actions following the tragedy caused his subjects, especially the aristocrats, to despise him terribly.

As the fifth Roman emperor and the last of the Julio-Claudian dynasty, Nero undoubtedly had big shoes to fill. The commoners initially favored him, and he showed signs of being a great ruler during the early years of his reign. It was only after his mother's death, according to ancient sources, that Nero began to unleash his tyrannical acts. The emperor knew he must act, so he opened the doors of his palace for his subjects to take shelter and prevented starvation by providing food supplies paid for from his own treasury. Nevertheless, the accusations soon reached his ears. Realizing he needed a scapegoat, Nero blamed the Christians and led the first Christian persecution. They were severely tortured and executed in public. Though houses were rebuilt and restoration projects for the city were launched, Nero also had something else in mind.

The emperor focused more on building the Golden House, a sumptuous palace for himself where he planned on hosting wild parties and lavish banquets. To fund the work needed to realize his dreams, Nero abused his power. He imposed high taxes on his people, seized lands owned by the aristocrats, imposed heavier tributes on the empire's provinces, and devalued the Roman currency. This, however, was the last straw. Conspiracies and rebellions began to occur the following year. Nero was announced public enemy and lost the support of everyone around him, resulting in his suicide in 68 CE.

Though Rome applauded upon hearing news of Nero's death, the empire was far from steady. It was ruled by several incompetent rulers (each ruling only for months) until Vespasian finally took the mantle in December 69 CE. The Flavian emperor planned to erase the traces Nero and his failed successors had left all over Rome, so he gave the land once taken by the dead emperor back to the Romans. To please the Roman citizens, Vespasian made a symbolic gesture; he passed a decree that a grand amphitheater would be built on the site of Nero's Golden House. Here, his people could enjoy nearly endless gladiatorial games and other performances.

The grand project took place sometime in 70-72 CE and would be completed almost a decade later. However, Vespasian never lived long enough to witness the completion of the grand amphitheater; the emperor is believed to have fallen ill and died in 79 CE. His eldest son and successor, Titus, continued his father's ambition and oversaw the construction project to its completion. Initially known to the ancient Romans as the Flavian Amphitheatre, the structure is known today as the Colosseum.

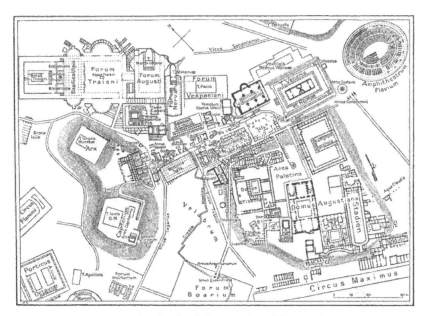
A map showing the Colosseum (top right corner).
https://commons.wikimedia.org/wiki/File:Map_of_downtown_Rome_during_the_Roman_Empire_large.png

Many had been waiting for the completion of the grand amphitheater. Seeing how intrigued his subjects were once they laid eyes on the final design of the Colosseum, Titus thought it would be fitting to hold a grand opening ceremony. The inauguration of the Colosseum took place in 80 CE, and it was indeed one of the most unforgettable events in the history of ancient Rome.

Ancient records state that the ceremony began with an elaborate procession of the emperor, who was fully adorned in his purple imperial regalia. Titus was also accompanied by senators, high-ranking officials, and members of the Roman elite, each showcasing their wealth and nobility through their garments.

A series of shows were organized to keep the citizens entertained. Titus had also announced a hundred days of gladiatorial games to commemorate the structure's completion. Venationes, or animal hunts, were also held; spectators would cheer in unison whenever the gladiators successfully slaughtered a beast. Apart from vicious fights and bloodied warriors, the opening of the Colosseum also included theatrical performances and music shows.

A depiction of the Colosseum minted on a coin dated from 80 CE.
Rc 13, CC BY-SA 3.0 <https://creativecommons.org/licenses/by-sa/3.0>, via Wikimedia Commons: https://commons.wikimedia.org/wiki/File:Colosseum_Ses_Titus_80AD.JPG

Just as anyone would have expected, the works on such a colossal amphitheater required extensive planning and engineering, especially since the structure was built on a site that was once an artificial lake within Nero's lavish garden. To commence construction, the Romans must first drain the lake. And so, they dug out a series of drains nearly eight meters beneath the ground to draw the water away from the site. Only then would they construct the foundation. To prevent the giant elliptical-shaped structure from collapsing, concrete foundations were carefully constructed deep underground. Apart from the popular Roman concrete, the Colosseum was also made of travertine stone, easily quarried from the ancient town of Albulae. The only problem was that the town was over thirty kilometers from Rome. So, the Romans constructed a road to ease the transportation of the travertine stones. Historians claim that over this newly-constructed road, the Romans (or their slaves) could move at least 240,000 carts daily.

Today, the overall shape of the Colosseum might appear circular and rather simple to some, but the structure has gone through countless episodes of destruction throughout the years. In its glory days, the Colosseum was considered one of the most complex structures ever built by human hands. The unnamed architects behind the wondrous structure carefully used extremely detailed mathematical calculations to shape every inch of the arches, vaults, and even the spectators' seats.

Upon completion, the Colosseum measured 188 meters long and 156 meters wide. The structure towered fifty-seven meters above ground and was divided into four stories. Within the Colosseum itself was not one but several centers. Impressively, the width of the auditorium and arena was the same as the structure's entire height. The amphitheater also featured eighty entrance arches; each measured exactly twenty Roman feet wide (equivalent to nearly six meters) and was built less than a meter apart. These arches were crucial to allowing a smooth flow of spectators to enter and exit the amphitheater. The arena itself had wooden floors, though they were covered by sand. To protect the cheering spectators from the burning sun, parts of the Colosseum were covered with canvas.

Ancient writings stated that the Colosseum could accommodate up to 50,000 people at once. While the gladiators and caged wild animals were placed in the hypogeum beneath the arena before the fights began, the spectators were seated according to their social classes. The more privileged the citizen was, the closer their seat to the arena. Unsurprisingly, the top tier, which provided the best view, was granted to the emperor. Those of the Roman courts and social elites were given seats on the highest tier, lower only than the emperor's box. The second tier was reserved for government officials and wealthy businessmen, while seating on the third tier was for ordinary Roman citizens. Women, the poor, and slaves, on the other hand, sat only on wooden benches on the lowest ground with limited views.

The remnants of the tiered seating.
Sean MacEntee from Monaghan, Ireland, CC BY 2.0
<https://creativecommons.org/licenses/by/2.0>, via Wikimedia Commons:
https://commons.wikimedia.org/wiki/File:The_Colosseum_(9554989427).jpg

Gladiatorial games were indeed the Romans' favorite type of entertainment. The Colosseum would be swarmed by tens of thousands of citizens whenever an emperor decided to host a game—usually to celebrate a triumph. However, the Colosseum was not just used for gladiatorial fights and mock naval battles; priests also used the amphitheater to conduct religious ceremonies—typically done before the start of a gladiatorial games. When there was supposed to be a sacrificial ceremony, the Romans would install a marble altar in the middle of the arena. Whether it was done as a dedication to Diana, Jupiter, or even Mars, it was common for the ceremony to include animal sacrifice. The sex of the sacrificial animal must correspond to the sex of the gods they were honoring. Sources also suggest that even the colors of the animals varied: white animals were sacrificed only in the name of the gods residing in the upper celestial world, while black ones were reserved for gods of the underworld.

The Colosseum arena, showing the hypogeum.

Though the Colosseum was an important structure in the Roman world, it would soon witness its slow abandonment. The spread of Christianity in Rome played a vital role in disusing the glorious amphitheater. As more Romans openly embraced Christianity, they began to deem gladiatorial contests as a form of entertainment that was opposite their beliefs. The fights were also heavily intertwined with Roman paganism; hence, it would be fitting that they were stopped. And so, the popularity of gladiatorial contests declined when Rome entered the fifth century CE. Eventually, the shows disappeared.

Without the gladiatorial fights, the Colosseum plunged into a period of disuse. The structure was then forced to endure several natural disasters resulting in its damage (though the amphitheater already appeared mutilated due to the Romans' constant harvest of its marble, used in constructing other buildings). A major earthquake then hit the Colosseum sometime in 443 CE, but it was the one in 1349 CE that severely damaged the structure. The Colosseum lost a huge chunk of its southern wall, ruining its perfect elliptical shape. The appearance of the Colosseum we see today resulted from this earthquake.

The Colosseum today.

Restoring such major damage would cost the empire a fortune. Sadly, the empire was on the verge of collapse: the Romans were crippled with political challenges and economic and financial disasters. When the Western Roman Empire fell into the hands of the Germanic barbarian tribes, the once magnificent Colosseum fell into complete neglect and abandonment.

Although the Colosseum no longer holds shows and performances, and its facade is permanently damaged, the amphitheater remains a symbol of ancient Roman engineering and culture. Its architectural design and intriguing history never fail to captivate visitors. Indeed, the structure was heavily neglected in ancient times. But today, efforts have been exhausted to preserve and restore it so that it will last for centuries to come. In the modern world, the Colosseum no longer serves as a site of vicious fights or sacrificial rituals; instead, it stands as evidence of the remarkable achievements of ancient Rome and its enduring legacy in architectural history.

Chapter 4 - From Sand to Sea: Gladiatorial Combat and Naval Reenactments at the Colosseum

It was a day unlike any other in Rome. The nobles had left the comfort of their domus (a type of Roman house owned by the rich), the farmers had hung their sickles earlier than usual, and even the slaves had earned their rest just for today. It was a day when a grand gladiatorial game would soon take place under the massive sponsorship of the reigning emperor.

As the sun reached its zenith, the amphitheater was already filled to the brim. Thousands of spectators had taken their seats, with the wealthy given the best of views, while slaves and women occupied the lowest seats where their views were often restricted. Unlike in a modern theater where the air is quiet, the Roman amphitheater was the opposite. Amidst the grand arches and towering walls, the spectators let out a series of voices and cheers that blended into a deafening roar, sounds that clearly expressed their excitement for the game to begin.

The atmosphere grew even more restless when trumpets were blared, announcing the arrival of the emperor, fully adorned with a wreath on his head and a purple toga hugging his old yet stiff figure. With his arrival came the commencement of the gladiatorial games, which resulted in a round of unsynchronized applause and cheers from the thousands of spectators. Then, the gates at the far end of the arena were cracked open, followed by the sounds of clashing armor and heavy weapons dragged through the dry sand.

The cheers continued as the Romans saw two gladiators stepping out of the wooden gates. One was taller and bigger than the other, though each had a formidable figure. Their bodies had been covered in oil, highlighting their muscular frames from years of hardcore training.

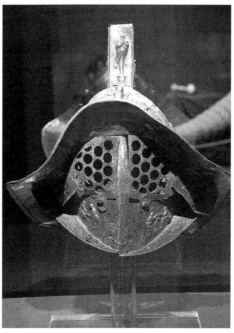

A gladiator helmet found in Pompeii.
Carole Raddato from FRANKFURT, Germany, CC BY-SA 2.0
<https://creativecommons.org/licenses/by-sa/2.0>, via Wikimedia Commons:
https://commons.wikimedia.org/wiki/File:Gladiator_helmet_found_in_Pompeii_and_richly_dec
orated_with_scenes_of_Greek_mythology,_Gladiators_%E2%80%93_Death_and_Triumph_at_t
he_Colosseum_exhibition,_Museum_und_Park_Kalkriese_(9618142634).jpg

The taller one was equipped with a gladius (a short sword best for quick slashes) and a shield, while the other wielded a long trident. When it was time to fight, the two vicious gladiators circled each other, their eyes locked in a deadly stare—perhaps to find each other's vulnerabilities. This was the moment the amphitheater went silent as the crowd held their breath, waiting for the first strike. After a few moments of observation, the gladiator with the trident used his agility and lunged forward, hoping he could at least thrust his godly weapon into his opponent's thigh. The other gladiator, however, was popular for his quick reflexes; he managed to dodge the attack.

Then, the crowds erupted in anticipation, each bellowing their support of their chosen champion—some even placed bets on which gladiator would fall on that day. The next few moments were filled with metal ringing against metal and armor clattering as the gladiators parried, dodged, and counterattacked their opponent. Whenever there was a successful attack and a splatter of blood touched the ground, the spectators let aloud gasps or cheers.

It did not take long for the clean and oiled torsos of the gladiators to be marked with bloody cuts and bruises. Yet, they continued to fight with unyielding determination, hoping to see the light of day again tomorrow. With every blow, the cheers grew louder, accompanied by groans and applause.

The finale came when one gladiator successfully seized an opportunity he had been calculating since the fight started. His opponent might have had a bigger figure, allowing him to attack with force, but his weight had tired him too fast. And so, without hesitation, the one armed with a trident quickly disarmed his opponent, sending his sword spiraling through the air, followed by a strike in the legs. The unarmed gladiator fell to his knees. The crowd erupted in a collective gasp, their excitement reaching a fever pitch.

A depiction of a gladiatorial fight.
https://commons.wikimedia.org/wiki/File;Jean-Leon_Gerome_Pollice_Verso.jpg

Although already considered victorious, the gladiator had one last choice: he must determine whether to let his opponent survive another day, despite them being friends before they were forcefully brought to the arena. He held his trident high, his posture poised to deliver the final blow. However, instead of delivering the death blow, the victorious gladiator extended his hand, offering mercy to his opponent. The spectators erupted into loud applause combined with shouts of admiration for his actions. Though many enjoyed the finale, some were dissatisfied, as if not enough blood was spilled.

Gladiatorial fights were not always popular in ancient Rome. While certain scholars believe that gladiatorial games were borrowed from the Etruscans, who usually held them in honor of their gods, others claim that the Roman games did not merely serve as entertainment but as rituals in funeral ceremonies. However, over time, these games grew in popularity and eventually became a form of public entertainment typically held ten to twelve times a year. Before the construction of the Colosseum, gladiatorial games were held in various venues across ancient Rome. Not limited to only amphitheaters, the games were also held in open spaces within a bustling city.

Most of the time, amphitheaters during the pre-Colosseum era were not built permanently on a specific site; instead, they were temporary structures that could be constructed at any time and dismantled once the games were over. However, when the Romans completed the Theatre of Pompey, temporary amphitheaters became a thing in the past. This was also when Roman amphitheaters were brought to a new height. Commissioned by none other than Gnaeus Pompeius Magnus, better known as Pompey the Great, in 55 BCE, it was Rome's first ever permanent amphitheater made of stone.

Given its massive structure—it was considered the largest in Rome at that time—the Theatre of Pompey was not only used as a gladiatorial arena but also designed for theatrical performances, speeches, and various other cultural events. The amphitheater also grew infamous towards the end of the Roman Republic; this was where the most powerful Roman general and dictator, Julius Caesar, got stabbed twenty-three times by his fellow senators.

Rome was indeed regarded as one of the most colossal empires in the ancient world. The Romans lived, endured, and loved wars. They were known for their military prowess and merciless punishments for those who wronged them. Enemies who refused to bow down to them were put to death, while those had been captured or surrendered were put in chains and sold as slaves.

However, captives, slaves, and prisoners of war deemed strong and possessing mighty figures were put on a different path; these people were sent to gladiatorial schools, where they were trained extensively in combat techniques. Instead of serving their time behind bars (or worse, being slaughtered), these chosen people were expected to put on thrilling performances before crowds of thousands. But, of course, not all gladiators were forced or condemned individuals; many men willingly registered their names as gladiators for personal reasons. Some were looking for fame, while others were searching for a way to escape poverty. At some point, even women joined and fought in the arena.

Contrary to popular belief, a gladiatorial game did not always end with the last person standing. In fact, the outcome of a gladiatorial fight depended on the event organizers, sponsors, or at times, the cheering crowds. Becoming a gladiator warrior did not mean certain death. After all, the gladiator schools owned the fighters, and the cost of hiring a new one to replace the dead was unsurprisingly expensive. Gladiators who survived numerous fights and had served their contracts, on the other hand, were rewarded with freedom. Some gained fortune and fame, while those who wished to stay in the industry were allowed to become trainers.

Perhaps the title of the most renowned figure in the history of gladiatorial combat goes to the Thracian Spartacus. History wrote that Spartacus once served the Eternal City as a soldier but was sold into slavery for his military desertion. He was brought to Capua, where he was forced to train as a gladiator. Not content with his fate, Spartacus and a few other gladiators attempted to escape. This event quickly boiled into something the Romans could never forget. Their attempt was successful, and this act was followed by a series of revolts against the Roman Republic.

Spartacus gathered a small group of followers who had long suffered under the republic. Over time, the number of his followers swelled into an army, allowing them to challenge the might of Rome. With sufficient training and strategies, combined with higher authorities who underestimated their power, Spartacus and his troops successfully defeated several Roman legions. The Roman court soon tasted the impending dangers they would face as long as Spartacus was alive. Only then did they begin to take drastic measures to quell the rebellion.

By 71 BCE, two years following the start of the revolt, Spartacus and his forces were finally defeated at the hands of the Roman general Marcus Licinius Crassus. Though the fate of Spartacus himself remains uncertain—some suggest he died in battle, while others claim he was captured and executed—the rebellion never had a chance to repeat their successes. Rome never saw another revolt led by discontented gladiators. Though the Roman court gained victory, it was Spartacus who successfully gained immortality; he quickly became a symbol of resistance and freedom, leaving a lasting impact on the Roman psyche.

An illustration depicting Spartacus' supposed death.
https://commons.wikimedia.org/wiki/File:Tod_des_Spartacus_by_Hermann_Vogel.jpg

Nevertheless, the gladiatorial games continued to be immensely popular among the Romans. They eventually became more than a form of entertainment. Especially after the completion of the Colosseum in 80 CE, gladiatorial games were held more often as a display of power and authority of the reigning emperor. The Colosseum also allowed gladiatorial games to reach new heights of extravagance and brutality. Animal hunts became more common, and grand mock naval battles became increasingly popular.

Also known to the ancient Romans as naumachia, mock naval battles were not exclusively held after the completion of the Colosseum. In fact, their origins can be traced to Julius Caesar, who held the first recorded naumachia in 46 BCE. To celebrate his military victories, Caesar had his subjects create a large-scale artificial lake by flooding a basin near the Tiber River. Here, the mock battle took place, featuring fully equipped ships and thousands of combatants reenacting one of Caesar's naval battles on a grand scale. Caesar was not the only one fond of expensive performances. The first Roman emperor, Augustus, also held his very own naumachia in 2 BCE to celebrate the opening of the Temple of Mars Ultor.

The grandest naumachia ever held, however, was the one hosted by Emperor Claudius in 52 BCE as part of an opening ceremony of a canal later used to dry the Fucine Lake. According to the ancient historian Suetonius, Claudius' naumachia had nearly a hundred ships—triremes and quadriremes—prepared for the mock battle, with over 19,000 slaves dressed in armor, ready (though not willingly) to fight each other.

Naumachiae continued to entertain the Romans after the completion of the Colosseum. With its innovative engineering, the colossal amphitheater could hold elaborate water-based performances. Although the exact methods used to flood and drain the Colosseum's vast arena remain a mystery, many historians and archaeologists have proposed their own theories. One suggestion is that the water was diverted from nearby giant aqueducts into the arena; others proposed that the arena's elaborate drainage system was utilized to flood the space—its sluiced gates were used to flood and drain the arena. Regardless of the technique, the Colosseum was filled with water measuring about five feet deep.

A painting depicting the Roman naumachia.
https://commons.wikimedia.org/wiki/File:La_naumaquia-Ulpiano_Checa.JPG

Since the depth was limited, the Romans had to build miniature boats with flat bottoms, each measuring seven to fifteen meters long. Designed meticulously to resemble the actual warships used in battles, the boats were manned by gladiators in armor who would engage in full-strength combat as if they were indeed fighting for their empire in an actual battle.

It is unknown how many naumachiae were ever held in the Colosseum, as few detailed written records survived the test of time. Emperor Titus was said to have hosted one during the grand opening of the Colosseum. Given Titus' penchant for extravagant displays, it is safe to assume that his naumachia was spectacular, captivating tens of thousands with its scale and spectacle.

Naumachiae never failed to attract huge crowds. However, this form of Roman entertainment was unfortunately rare due to its exorbitant cost. It eventually declined in popularity as time passed. Sources suggested that the last naumachia held in the Colosseum took place in 89 CE and was sponsored by Emperor Domitian. To save money, naumachiae were then commonly staged in lakes as they were before. Since it was less expensive to host them in lakes, naumachiae were probably held there more frequently, though they lacked grandeur. Because of this, the Romans gradually lost interest, favoring other forms of entertainment such as the bloody gladiatorial games, chariot racing, and theatrical performances typically held on land.

Chapter 5 - Petra: A Wonder with Mysterious Beginnings

History has always been entangled with mystery. Archaeologists and historians may find new artifacts that could lead them to a new discovery or perhaps unlock a better understanding of a certain period and civilizations of the past. However, most of these discoveries grant us more questions than answers. The ancient city of Petra is one of the best examples of a wonder that still plagues historians with mysteries.

Many centuries ago, trade was considered a crucial part of the economies and development of ancient civilizations. A small kingdom could bloom into a full-fledged empire through successful trading. Those who held power and controlled the many trade routes and ports had the utmost ability to control the entire world. Spices, exotic animals, gems, and silk were commonly traded throughout this period, but incense quickly grew popular and soon became an important commodity in the ancient world. Not only limited to religious ceremonies, incense was also used in various other ways. Some, especially the ancient Egyptians, used it while embalming the dead and mummifying them. Believed to have healing properties, incense was also valued as a form of medication. Others used it to enhance the taste of wine. As the demand for incense boomed, kingdoms that controlled the incense trade were guaranteed centuries of pouring wealth.

The ancient kingdom of Saba (or Sheba, according to biblical and Quranic references), for one, quickly became the wealthiest kingdom in southern Arabia due to its monopoly on the incense trade. Two of the most valuable types of incense at the time were frankincense and myrrh, which were cultivated from the trees that typically grew in the desert regions of Oman and Yemen. From these regions, the incense was transported by camel caravans via the incense route, which stretched over two thousand kilometers, linking southern Arabia far into the Mediterranean world. Once the cargo arrived at Gaza, a busy port city at the end of the Mediterranean coast, the precious incense would be prepared for shipment via sea to enter the markets of Greece, Rome, Egypt, and beyond.

Though the rewards were exceptionally high, the journey through the incense route was beyond challenging. Not only did the caravans face attacks from bandits lurking in the shadows of night, but traders must also brave the perilous desert with the threats imposed by mother nature herself. Sandstorms were common, and many perished due to limited resources, especially water. However, one tribe was cunning enough to devise a solution to the obstacles that often slow the movements of their caravans. They were known as the Nabateans.

The origin of the Nabateans is rather obscure. They were thought to be literate, but few historical records produced by the tribe still survive. The Nabateans began appearing on written records sometime in the fourth century BCE, though it is plausible they existed long before that. Nevertheless, historians claim that before establishing their kingdom, the Nabateans were Arabian nomads who came all the way from the Negev Desert. Despite the Nabateans' obscure background, we can be sure that, given their constant move around the region, they familiarized themselves with the natural topography and geography of the incense route.

Just as traversing through the incense route was not an easy feat, a one-way journey to reach the port of Gaza took a minimum of sixty-five days, with merchants stopping at a different city each night. Within these cities, merchants were given a chance to rest without worrying about bandits stealing their cargo; they could conduct business and barter their goods in exchange for water. Water was indeed a crucial supply to the merchants, as it was used to sustain them on their dangerous journey until they reached the next city, where the same process would be repeated. Although these overnight stops inevitably delayed their movement toward their final destination in Gaza, it was absolutely necessary to do so.

The trading business, at that time, was undoubtedly competitive, and the Nabateans were well aware of it. The only way to emerge on top was to defeat time itself. The Nabateans planned to limit their overnight stops, thus cutting their travel time to reach the port. To ensure they always had enough water to sustain their journey, the Nabateans dug cisterns along the route and filled them with precious rainwater. These cisterns were then carefully concealed to avoid other Arabian tribes accessing them. Subtle signs that only the Nabateans would recognize were left along the way to point to the cisterns. With these controlled water supplies, the Nabateans could navigate back and forth along the incense route with ease and in an impressively shorter amount of time.

Through their clever innovation, the Nabateans had successfully established themselves as the preeminent traders of the Arabian Peninsula. Once known as an enigmatic nomadic tribe with an unknown background, the Nabateans amassed so much wealth from their trading activities that they were able to assert their dominance and gained control over several integral cities along the incense route. Haluza, Mamshit, Avdat, and Shivta were some of the cities under the Nabateans that were greatly improved to accommodate the traveling merchants. Forts were then constructed to ensure protection for traders who stopped by. Safety, however, was not without a price; traders who desired the luxury of a peaceful night's sleep had to pay a nominal tax.

After being rewarded with such great fortune and crowned as the masters of trade, the Nabateans left their past. From a tribe of wandering merchants, they transformed into a prosperous kingdom that laid the foundation of Petra, their first capital city in southern Jordan, which has earned a place in modern times as one of the seven wonders of the new world. Historians and archaeologists alike cannot yet determine when the construction of Petra took place, but surviving records claim that the city had already achieved fame sometime in the fourth century BCE.

When the Nabateans first planned to establish Petra, finding a strategic location was at the top of the list. They valued their fortune in the trade economy, so it was only wise for them to choose a site along the Incense Trade Route where numerous caravans would pass through day and night. However, many may have underestimated the city. Though the site was strategic, the city was built on a barren desert with nothing but rocky cliffs and a scorching sun burning in the skies. But the Nabateans were highly innovative and gifted builders. They engineered a system to harness the rainwater that came in winter to sustain their entire city: a network of cisterns was carefully constructed to capture the trapped rainwater and supply it to the many sites of the city, including its grandest temples, houses, theatres, fountains, and other public buildings. Those rocky cliffs, on the other hand, proved useful. They acted as natural fortifications against enemies and bandits who dreamed of benefiting from stealing precious cargo brought in by the merchants.

The Egyptians built pyramids using a combination of limestones and mud bricks, while the Romans were famous for their marble structures and monuments. Although the Nabateans were also exposed to these architectural elements (largely due to the influences brought in by the traveling merchants), they chose to discard the idea of designing their city with traditional building materials in favor of a more audacious approach none had ever attempted before. Instead of quarrying limestones and transporting stone slabs from one town to another, the Nabateans used their natural surroundings. Using the resolute sandstone rocks and cliffs as their canvas, the Nabateans carved their city from scratch. Not merely builders but also exceptional artists, the Nabateans successfully chiseled away at the rocks and sculptured the rough cliffs into some of the most stunning structures unlike any other. These hand-carved buildings were also sturdy enough to withstand earthquakes.

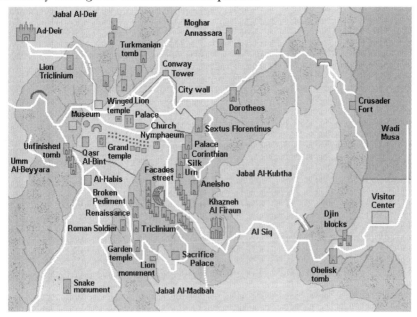

The map of Petra.
https://commons.wikimedia.org/wiki/File:Karta_Petra.PNG

Though built on an empty and dry desert, the city once appeared to be not so much rose red but bright green thanks to the Nabateans' sophisticated network of cisterns, aqueducts, and pipelines that efficiently carried water to irrigate the city's lush gardens, groves, orchards, fountains, and swimming pools. Combining this with its strategic location along the trade route, Petra soon became a bustling trade hub that welcomed merchants and travelers from all over the globe. At its peak, Petra housed over 30,000 citizens of various origins, some of whom were immigrants all the way from Rome, Egypt, Greece, Syria, and Judea.

Once through the narrow gorge called Siq, the main entrance of the ancient city, one could feast one's eyes on the unbelievable sight of the Al-Khazneh, recognized by many historians and scholars from both ancient and modern times as one of the most intricate structures in the desert city. Carved directly into the solid face of the sandstone cliff with exceptional precision and attention to detail, the Al-Khazneh (Arabic for "the Treasury") successfully combined the intricate architectural designs of the indigenous Nabateans with a unique blend of Hellenistic and Egyptian styles. It rose at least forty-three meters above ground and was adorned with elaborate friezes, ornate columns, and decorative motifs, each hand-carved to perfection by the ancient Nabateans using only chisels, hammers, and other hand tools.

The narrow passage, Siq, that leads to Petra.
JoTB, CC BY-SA 3.0 <https://creativecommons.org/licenses/by-sa/3.0>, via Wikimedia Commons: https://commons.wikimedia.org/wiki/File:Al-Siq_2.jpg

The purpose of Al-Khazneh, however, remains a subject of debate among archaeologists and historians. Some believe it once served as a ceremonial tomb or mausoleum for important Nabatean figures, most possibly a respected king or queen. The funerary urn crowning the structure further supports this claim. Legend has it that this structure was also used to store precious treasures once belonging to an unknown Egyptian pharaoh. These are nothing more than legends passed down from generation to generation; no treasure has ever been found hidden within the structure. We can never be sure whether there was no treasure or it was already seized by those before us.

The Treasury.

At Petra, one can also find Ad-Deir ("the Monastery"), another of the several Nabatean wonders. Compared to Al-Khazneh, Ad-Deir was constructed to appear slightly bigger; it rose forty-five meters high and had a width of nearly fifty meters. Based on the carvings of crosses on the walls within the sandstone structure, it is suggestive that Ad-Deir was converted into a church during the era of the Byzantines.

The Ad-Deir.

Just as in the glorious times when Petra was flourishing, as modern-day visitors wind up the ancient streets, they encounter another impressive series of tombs hewn into the rough surface of the rocky massif, Jabal al-Khubtha. These royal tombs—namely, the Urn Tomb, the Silk Tomb, and the Corinthian Tomb—exhibit elaborate facades that precisely reflect the unimaginable wealth of the Nabatean elites buried there.

The Royal Tombs of Petra.

Along the path and south of the Colonnaded Street of Petra was the Great Temple, another of the many architectural marvels hand-carved by the patient Nabateans. Presumably constructed in the early first century CE, the complex served as either a religious site or an administrative center. As with the rest of the structures uncovered in Petra, debate on the exact purpose of the Great Temple has been ongoing. The temple's grandeur and monumental size, however, show significant signs that it was indeed built as a dedication to the Nabatean deities. This site could also be where important ceremonies and gatherings were held. Though what remains of the Great Temple are only colossal columns, remnants of the expansive staircase, and several chambers, the site never fails to leave visitors completely awe-struck.

Ruins of the Great Temple.

Not limited to only the Al-Khazneh, Ad-Deir, the Royal Tombs, and the Great Temple, the rest of the structures scattered throughout Petra's sprawling landscape have proven the rich culture of the Nabateans and their architectural genius. Though forgotten by many following the years when the Romans renamed themselves the Byzantines, Petra was not planning to be buried beneath the dust again. Declared a UNESCO World Heritage Site along with six other wonders of the new world, it will be a long time–or never–before Petra can be forgotten again.

Chapter 6 - Petra: The Envy of the Ancient World's Superpowers

The year was 323 BCE, and the people of Ancient Macedonia were mourning. Their king and the mighty conqueror, Alexander the Great, had just passed away after battling a serious illness that had left him in bed day and night. Though he had a wife—who was pregnant with his first child—the conqueror never named a successor to continue his legacy. And so, his vast empire, which spanned from Greece to Egypt, Persia, and a portion of India, was divided among his most powerful comrades: Ptolemy, Seleucus, Cassander, and Antigonus. These generals each gained control over different territories and often waged war with each other. However, Antigonus was widely considered the greatest success of the four.

Antigonus had been swaying his sword on the battlefield and commanding the Macedonian phalanx since the reign of King Philip II, the father of Alexander the Great. Beginning his career as a mere soldier, Antigonus rose through the ranks and eventually became one of Philip's most trusted advisors. It was also during a battle under Philip's rule that Antigonus received a terrible blow across his face. As a result, he lost his right eye; after that, he was known as Antigonus the One-Eyed.

With or without his right eye, Antigonus was never known to back down; he continued leading his troops in many more campaigns, each far more dangerous than the previous. After Philip's death, Antigonus continued to serve under Alexander and was appointed as a general in the army who was absolutely instrumental in securing Alexander's victories in both Persia and Egypt.

As an ambitious and ruthless ruler, Antigonus dreamed of reuniting the great empire once established by Alexander, and he planned to rule it alone. And so, he began expanding his domain, the Antigonid dynasty. With careful planning and execution, he quickly swept across Syria and conquered the Mediterranean coast. Military campaigns were no doubt expensive, and his rapid expansion had, of course, drained his coffers. Thus, he decided to hungrily shift his focus to Petra—a city he deemed extremely wealthy—that could be greatly useful for his empire's conquest.

Sometime in 312 BCE, Antigonus sent one of his trusted generals, Athenaeus, to the dry lands of the Nabateans with a mission to secure their vast resources and riches. Backed up by four thousand light foot soldiers, some of whom had served under Alexander and six hundred horsemen, Athenaeus marched out of Judea and into the merciless desert en route to plunder as much Nabatean wealth as his animals could carry.

It took them three days before they could set eyes on the Rose City. Noticing how busy Petra could be during the day, Athenaeus ordered his troops to set camp and wait for nightfall. As soon as the dark shadows of night covered the entire rock-cut city, Athenaeus and his army made a move. Under the cover of darkness, they stormed the quiet city. There was little resistance, as most Nabatean men had gone on the road to conduct business. Women and children were caught by surprise by the attack. The silence of the dark night was replaced by screaming and pleas as the troops went into a frenzy; they looted all the riches they could find and obliterated those who dared to stand in their way.

Before word about their sudden attack could reach the traveling Nabatean men, Athenaeus and his men quickly loaded their horses and carts with as much loot as they could plunder. Ancient sources state that they left Petra with countless precious trade goods, including frankincense, myrrh, and nearly fourteen tons of silver. Frightened women and children were also taken and put in shackles with the intention of selling them as slaves.

Content with all the fortune they had amassed from the easy ambush, Athenaeus and his men were confident they had accomplished their mission. And so, they set up another camp about thirty-six kilometers away from Petra, where they spent the night. One little mistake they overlooked, however, was the ones who were left wounded in the city.

A few hours after Athenaeus' departure, the first few Nabatean men arrived in Petra. They were, of course, beyond surprised by the sight of their city. Their homes and holy temples were ransacked, and their families were nowhere to be found. At first, these men had zero idea of the culprit behind this tragedy. That was, until they started tending to the wounded. Fighting the pain inflicted by their wounds, the survivors told the Nabatean men of Athenaeus' attack. This information no doubt stoked the flames of anger and vengeance. In a matter of hours, the Nabatean men had armed themselves and mounted their camels, ready to set out and track down the cowardly invaders. As they rode through nearby settlements and villages, they rallied more and more warriors to their cause, swelling their numbers to eight thousand armed camel riders.

Athenaeus and his men had no idea what was coming for them. They spent the night sleeping with little thought of possible retaliation. As they were sleeping soundly, their prisoners were said to have successfully sneaked out of the camp undetected. The eight thousand camel riders arrived at the camp by nightfall. Perhaps learning from the Antigonids, they used the cover of darkness and laid a surprise attack. Using javelins, the Nabateans slaughtered their enemies. Those who were deep asleep died without having the chance to defend themselves, while those who had their swords were quickly dealt with. Out of all, only fifty horsemen managed to escape the attack—though they, too, were terribly injured. With this victory, the Nabateans successfully reclaimed what was theirs; all of the stolen wealth was brought back to the city along with the captured prisoners, women, and children.

Despite their prowess in battle, the Nabateans were, in fact, peaceful people and had no desire for further bloodshed. Seeking to avoid any unnecessary conflict, they wrote a letter in Aramaic (the region's lingua franca) and sent it to Antigonus, explaining the circumstances that had led to the slaughter of Athenaeus and his men. To their surprise, Antigonus showed signs of understanding and excused them for the killings. Though he was trying to project his image as a calm ruler during this exchange, Antigonus had no intention of leaving the Nabateans alone. He knew they were a proud people who valued their independence above all, so the Antigonid king sought to placate them with promises of peace and security. In his reply, he assured the

Nabateans that there would be no war following the massacre.

Although partly relieved by Antigonus' response, the Nabateans could not afford to be caught off-guard again. Despite the king's assurances, they remained skeptical and maintained their guard, stationing sentries along the borders and atop the cliffs to watch for any sign of foreign aggression.

Their suspicions proved to be well-founded. Antigonus, determined to succeed where Athenaeus had failed, dispatched his son Demetrius with an army of another four thousand skilled soldiers to Petra. However, the Nabatean watchmen were quick to spot the Antigonid army from afar and immediately set fire to warning beacons placed on hilltops throughout the region. They gathered their families and valuables and retreated to a stony fortress that historians believe was carved into Petra's highest point, the mountain Umm Al-Biyara.

Learning of their retreat, Demetrius and his soldiers laid an assault on the fortress, but its natural defenses made the attack impossible. The narrow crevices leading up to the fortress would be deadly for his soldiers to navigate, and besieging it was not an option as the Nabateans had their own secret supplies of water. Demetrius was, indeed, on the brink of defeat, but he refused to return empty-handed.

Unbeknownst to the Antigonids, the Nabateans were not only cunning fighters but also gifted in the art of negotiations. As Demetrius led his army in another attempt to breach the impregnable fortress, a shrewd Nabatean stepped forward to speak. He first questioned Antigonus' motive for invading them, arguing that their city was built far into the desert and posed no threat to anyone. He stated that his people were not planning to harm others, as they wished only to carry on with their lives in peace. The man then laid out his negotiation terms: the Nabateans would gift the Antigonids with generous riches if they retreated to where they belonged and maintained a friendly relationship with the Nabateans.

The Antigonids, whose supplies began to deplete, had no choice but to agree to the offer. Demetrius accepted the handsome gifts and led his troops back to their homeland, though he was not pleased with the outcome. Upon receiving the reports of the failed invasion, Antigonus was said by the historian Diodorus to have expressed his anger towards his son. Despite returning from Arabia much richer, the Antigonids were far from victory. Antigonus claimed that his son had allowed the barbaric

Nabateans to grow even bolder. Nevertheless, the Antigonids unintentionally stayed true to their promise after all; eventually, Antigonus was forced to abandon his plans on Petra as he needed to settle internal matters.

The Nabateans and their Rose City were spared from war and bloodshed. But, as their wealth grew each year, they attracted another colossal power of the ancient world: this time, it was the Roman Empire, which had just expanded its realm to Egypt.

One of the reasons behind their plan to conquer the Nabateans was the rich incense fields of Arabia. The Romans were religious people and one of the largest consumers of incense. Frankincense was burned in their many temples, and the Romans also constantly used myrrh as part of their religious rituals. As the empire experienced rapid expansion and its population grew, it was estimated that over a million kilograms of frankincense were imported from Arabia. In the eyes of the reigning emperor, Augustus Caesar, the cost of the import was draining his coffers, especially when the Nabateans had imposed a 25 percent tax on the goods. And so, Augustus sought ways to minimize his vast empire's spending; instead of negotiating, he planned to get his hands on the incense trade route.

However, one problem loomed over his head—the Romans were not perfectly familiar with the territories of Southern Arabia. Therefore, Augustus sent Aelius Gallus, his trusted prefect in charge of Roman Egypt, to explore the lay of the land and establish new trade routes that would connect them to the locals. Equipped with only a small force, Aelius Gallus led the expedition until it was met with a warm welcome by the Nabateans.

Surprisingly, the Nabateans maintained friendly communication with the Romans—they even provided one of their own as a guide for the Romans' exploration. According to the Greek geographer and historian Strabo, instead of having their guards up, the Romans were pleased with the supposed cooperation of the Nabateans and let themselves be guided by one of the locals sent by the Nabatean king. Little did they know, their guide was not merely a humble man who knew his map. Introducing himself as Syllaeus, the man held a high political position in the court of the Nabatean government. Before meeting with the Romans, who were more than eager to continue their expedition, Syllaeus had been strictly tasked by his king to do nothing but two things: he was to put on a mask and appear cooperative to the Romans while at the same time ensuring the expedition went south.

Syllaeus was undoubtedly put in a dangerous position. One wrong step, and he would face the wrath of the colossal empire. If he failed to mislead the Romans, Syllaeus might have his head served on a silver platter by the Nabatean king. Nevertheless, Syllaeus accomplished his tasks. He used the trust the Romans had in him and guided them through a long, perilous journey along the coast of southern Arabia. There were easier routes to Petra usually used by Arab traders, but Syllaeus managed to conceal this information.

Many of Gallus' men succumbed to their deaths during the six-month journey. Their lives were either taken by serious diseases, heat stroke, fatigue, or poisonous herbs and tainted water consumed along the way. The Romans were most likely traveling in circles, though every once in a while, Syllaeus would lead them on the right course so that he would not raise their suspicions. Only when his forces were severely depleted did Gallus admit defeat and announce that he would return to the empire.

Without delaying a single minute, Aelius Gallus led what remained of his troops back home, retracing the steps they had taken using the guidance of Syllaeus. At some point during his retreat, Gallus finally realized he had been tricked—informed by his captives. He could have spent only two days to reach Petra, but Syllaeus had successfully extended the journey. It is uncertain when Syllaeus made his quiet escape—it is safe to assume Syllaeus was not present when the Romans realized his tricks—but the Romans had returned to Alexandria with nothing but a pair of empty hands.

The Nabateans and Petra were spared yet again following Syllaeus' tricks. Like centuries before, Petra enjoyed its independence as the Romans had their hands full with a series of civil wars. About a century later, they would return; by 106 CE, the Romans successfully paid their vengeance. Petra and its surrounding territories were invaded and annexed into the empire, which changed the province's name to Arabia Petraea. From this moment on, the Romans would rule Petra for 250 years.

The Roman annexation was the beginning of an end for Petra and the Nabateans. As Christianity began to spread widely across the Roman Empire, the use of incense deteriorated; thus, Petra no longer enjoyed being the most popular trade hub. The once glorious city was also affected by the Galilee earthquake in 363 CE, resulting in the destruction of nearly half of its magnificent structures.

Two years after the unforgettable natural disaster, Petra was forced to endure a siege by the Byzantines under Emperor Justinian I. The Nabateans' defeat put them in the hands of the Byzantines, who would rule over them for three hundred years. By the eighth century CE, Petra almost completely fell into disuse. Since its location was no longer considered strategically important, Petra was abandoned, with its remaining structures inhabited by only nomadic shepherds. As the nomads moved on, Petra was reclaimed by the dust of the desert—left forgotten and hidden from the eyes of the Europeans.

That was, until 1812 when the explorer John Lewis Burckhardt rediscovered the city. Since then, the stone city has been exclusively put onto the world stage of archeology. Countless scholars, historians, and archaeologists visited the site, studying and admiring the wondrous city of the Nabateans. Though no longer carrying the title of the wealthiest city, Petra's historical and cultural significance grew, forever solidifying its position as one of the world's most remarkable ancient cities. Its rose-colored sandstone structures, hidden passages and crevices, and awe-inspiring landscapes continue to captivate visitors, transporting them back to an era when Petra flourished as a thriving center of trade and culture.

Chapter 7 - The Arrival of the Portuguese along the Shores of Brazil

By the end of the 15th century CE, the world had just begun to witness the start of a transformative era. Known in historical terms as the Age of Discovery, this was a time when European nations actively embarked on multiple series of voyages and expeditions in search of new trade routes and wealth. Among the many explorers frequently scouring through the ocean were the Portuguese, whose exceptional maritime prowess had turned them into one of the most formidable powers in European history.

In the early 15th century CE, Portuguese explorers were put under the leadership of Prince Henry the Navigator; their aim was to explore the undiscovered coast of Africa. And so, once disembarked from the harbor and the heavy anchor hoisted, the Portuguese, with eyes filled with determination, set sail across the sea, advancing farther south than any previous expeditions held by other European superpowers. After enduring all sorts of challenges in the ocean, including storms, diseases, and perhaps a few equipment failures, the Portuguese successfully mapped a good portion of western Africa. In 1488, they finally witnessed a greater achievement: Bartolomeu Dias had successfully become the first European to sail around the southern tip of Africa, known as the Cape of Good Hope. His success brought European maritime expeditions to a greater height as, a decade later, another Portuguese explorer named Vasco da Gama found a passage to reach India. This allowed the Europeans to establish a direct sea connection with the vast markets of the East.

Apart from the Portuguese Empire, Spain never failed to showcase its exploration skills in the Age of Discovery. Once done with the Reconquista (the Reconquest of Spain), campaigns that involved countless wars spanning over seven centuries, the Spanish could finally shift their attention to expanding their realm. They were indeed hungry for more lands, resources, and attractive wealth, typically hidden in the Far East.

Among the many explorers and seafarers aboard the ships carrying the flags of European countries, one particular figure hailing from Italy dreamed of being the first to set foot on the shores of Asia. His name was Christopher Columbus. After years of calculations, studies, and observation of the endless ocean, Columbus arrived at a conclusion that not everyone would nod to: he claimed there was an easy passage to Asia. By sailing west across the Atlantic instead of going around Africa, he could reach Asia with minimal time and difficulties.

Confident in his calculations, Columbus first proposed the idea to the Portuguese, proposing they fund his expedition. They immediately refused to lend him their support. Not planning to give up, the Italian explorer turned to the Spanish monarchs—Ferdinand and Isabella—who agreed to a sponsorship.

And so, Columbus embarked on a mission to prove his claim and discover new parts of the globe. He sailed across the Atlantic in 1492 until he finally docked at a Caribbean island, believing he had just discovered a western trade route to India and China. Upon nearing land, he mistakenly claimed that he had arrived on the eastern shores of Asia.

Columbus returned to Spain to inform his sponsors of the New World he had set his eyes on. Christopher Columbus was widely regarded as the first European to set foot on the New World. However, few knew that the title had already been given to Leif Erikson, a Norse explorer whose adventure took place nearly half a millennium before Columbus' birth. Regardless, the news brought back by Columbus immediately sparked a colossal wave of excitement among the European powers as they began planning ways to capitalize and benefit from the new-found lands.

Following Columbus' voyage, representatives from Spain and Portugal gathered to discuss which indigenous lands of the new world were located in whose territory. To resolve the matter, the two European nations signed the Treaty of Tordesillas, which divided the newly discovered lands between the two powers. Through the treaty, they established an imaginary line called the Line of Demarcation, which divided the lands of the Americas into separate spheres of influence. While Spain was granted rights to explore lands west of the line, Portugal was given those to the east.

As such, King Manuel I of Portugal, who was driven by ambitions, wealth, and power, set his eyes on colonizing as many lands as possible on the east of the imaginary line. One of the lands that would soon be added to the list was none other than Brazil.

The following years were filled by a race of expeditions sent out by these two rival powers. In 1500 CE, a Portuguese expedition under the leadership of Pedro Alvares Cabral had just left Lisbon with an initial aim to reach the East Indies. Several historical accounts suggest that Cabral intended to retrace the steps taken by Vasco da Gama during his unforgettable voyage around the Cape of Good Hope. However, unprecedented storms and navigational errors soon foiled his plans. Cabral and his team of explorers veered off-course and eventually made landfall at a location known to us today as Porto Seguro in northern Brazil. While these sources clearly suggest that Cabral had no prior knowledge of Brazil's existence, many claimed his arrival was intentional.

Regardless of the claims, Cabral was said to have not jumped onto the shores of Porto Seguro right away. Upon noticing inhabitants going about their lives on the shores from a distance, Cabral gathered the captains of his three ships for a discussion. He then ordered the captain, Nicolau Coelho, who had earned a name in the maritime industry for his participation in Vasco da Gama's expedition to India, to travel ashore and make contact with the locals—perhaps to see whether the locals were hostile to foreign faces. Without question, Coelho did what he was asked, and, fortunately, the locals maintained friendly expressions. They exchanged gifts, and it was only after Coelho's return to his ship that Cabral ordered his fleet to dock at Porto Seguro.

In return for the Portuguese's friendly introduction, the locals were pleased to show them around, providing information about their tribes. Most were hunter-gatherers to whom the Europeans had assigned the collective label "Indians." Men in these groups sustained their diet by hunting big game animals, fishing, and foraging, while women were often engaged in small-scale agriculture. There were multiple tribes inhabiting the land—some of whom practiced cannibalism—and the one who made contact with Cabral is believed to have belonged to the Tupiniquim tribe.

Cabral did not prolong his stay in Brazil; the Portuguese remained not more than ten days before setting on another journey to obtain the lucrative possessions of Africa and India. At the moment, the Portuguese paid little attention to Brazil. They would only return to the coasts to get brazilwood, often used by the Europeans to produce valuable red dyes for luxury textiles. The Portuguese were actively engaged in trade with the Brazilian tribes, as they had to rely on them to extract the brazilwood from the dense jungle. In return, the tribes obtained mirrors, scissors, knives, and axes from the Europeans.

It was only when the precious wood caught the attention of the French that the Portuguese Crown began to take action. By that time, the presence of the French had grown tremendously. And so, in 1530, a Portuguese expedition was dispatched to Brazil to patrol the coast. Spearheaded by Martim Afonso de Sousa, the Portuguese expelled the French and eventually established their first colonial villages along the coast.

Certain scholars claim that Brazil was thought of more as a lucrative commercial asset than a region to be settled. However, the Portuguese Crown eventually figured that having Brazil serve only as a trading post was not ideal; thus, they began to get deeper into the region's organizational structure. To ensure Brazil was always under their close watch, the Portuguese introduced a system of hereditary captaincies in which the territories were divided and overseen by high-ranking officials well-connected to the Portuguese Crown. The Portuguese nobleman, Duarte Coelho, for instance, was granted Pernambuco, a region that prospered by the cultivation of sugarcane and cotton. On the other hand, São Vicente, the first permanent Portuguese settlement, soon became a hub for indigenous slave trafficking.

In 1549, Brazil was met with the arrival of Tomé de Sousa, who established a central government. Arriving along the shores with him were the Jesuit priests, a Catholic religious order tasked with spreading Christianity in Brazil.

The Jesuits worked to accomplish their mission almost as soon as they arrived in Brazil. They established "reductions," mission towns, across the many regions of Brazil. Converting the indigenous people of Brazil was undoubtedly easier said than done. And so, the Jesuits tried approaching them not only to introduce their religious teachings but also to improve their living conditions and their entire well-being. The Jesuits opened the reductions to all locals, providing medical assistance to those in need while introducing them to new agricultural techniques to enhance the production of their crops. The Jesuits believed that education was essential for a person's spiritual and intellectual development. Thus, apart from churches, they built a few schools, which were typically used by the missionaries to provide education to the children of both the indigenous tribes and Portuguese settlers.

However, the locals were not the only ones learning; the Jesuits also spent their days and nights perfecting their skills in the native languages spoken by the indigenous people. With fluency in their mother tongue, the Jesuits could translate religious texts for the locals to better understand their teachings.

The Jesuits received the utmost support from the Portuguese Crown; by spreading Christianity all over the territory, the Portuguese thought it would be easier to consolidate their power. Thus, the missionaries were given more than enough financial and logistical assistance and legal protection for their roles. New policies were also introduced to ensure not a single local was excluded from Catholic teachings. This policy encouraged the indigenous people to set up their dwellings close to the missions.

Of course, converting the people of the Brazilian territory was not a walk in the park; there were multiple challenges and conflicts the Jesuits were forced to deal with. Not all locals were content with the arrival of a religion completely new to them. Many refused to convert, preferring to cling to their spiritual beliefs and centuries-long cultural practices. Mere arguments and minor clashes between indigenous traditions and Catholic teaching sometimes became serious tensions and conflicts. The diseases brought in by the foreigners, combined with forced labor imposed by the Portuguese colonial enterprises, further led the locals to turn away from Catholicism.

Despite the issues and obstacles, the Jesuits eventually witnessed a significant change in Brazilian society. More indigenous populations gradually chose to embrace aspects of Catholicism, merging some of their traditional beliefs with Christian rituals and practices. The Jesuit missions prospered and turned into important centers of religious and cultural exchange.

Over the centuries, Christianity continued to bloom all over Brazil, eventually shaping the religious, cultural, and architectural landscape of the region. Four centuries following the first arrival of the Portuguese Jesuits, Brazil became the home to one of the most iconic symbols in Christianity. The statue of Christ the Redeemer would soon rest atop the highest peak of Rio de Janeiro, overseeing the land and ocean surrounding it.

Chapter 8 - Christ the Redeemer: Brazil's Symbol of Faith

During the 19th century, particularly in the 1850s, a local priest was the first to propose the idea of building a colossal Christian monument in Rio, the capital of Brazil at the time. His proposal was presented out of a desire to honor the royal family, specifically Princess Isabel, the daughter of Emperor Pedro II and Empress Teresa Cristina. Recognizing the importance of the statue—to serve as a tribute to the monarchy and to emphasize the presence of Christianity in Brazil—the priest also voiced the idea of erecting the statue on Mount Corcovado, which geographically provides a strong presence for the statue and ensures its visibility from various locations throughout Rio de Janeiro.

Unfortunately, the idea to build the Christian monument faced various obstacles that eventually led to its cancellation. Some of the problems were the lack of funding and the political changes most likely brought by the Proclamation of the Republic in 1889—the creation of a republican government after ending the Brazilian monarchy.

A view of Mount Corcovado before the construction of Christ the Redeemer.
https://commons.wikimedia.org/wiki/File:Corcovadoporferrez.jpg

However, following the end of World War I, the idea of building such a monumental statue was picked up again. This time, it was proposed by the Roman Catholic archdiocese in Rio. The leaders were concerned about the state of Brazilians, who were thought to have gradually lost their religious faith. And so, in 1923, t to realize the project's construction, the Brazilians held a fundraising campaign. Referred to as "Monument Week," the campaign was well-received by the people and successfully garnered half of what was required to lay the project's foundation. However, building such a grand structure was easier said than done; it was not until a few years later that the construction work could finally begin.

Although the exact number of people who worked on the construction was not historically documented in writing, it is safe to assume that the work required hundreds of hands. Nevertheless, it is worth noting that three key figures worked tirelessly year after year to turn the Catholics' vision into reality. These men were Heitor da Silva Costa, Gheorghe Leonida, and Paul Landowski.

Like any monument ever built, the process of designing the statue was extensive; the first few sketches of Christ of Redeemer went through several revisions before it reached its final form. Heitor was the one who had been working tirelessly to create the best design for the statue. At first, he envisioned the monument to appear extravagant in its pose; his first sketch was of Jesus clasping an enormous cross against his body and his other hand holding a globe. He also planned to have the statue face in the direction of the rising sun.

Unfortunately, for unspecified reasons, the design was scrapped. Some suggest the design was too complex for construction on top of a mountain; others put the blame on an insufficient budget. Nevertheless, Heitor eventually came up with another idea that earned the green light.

Primarily influenced by the Art Deco style first introduced in France in the early 1920s, Heitor drew inspiration from the radio antennas that stop atop Mount Corcovado. He was further advised by the artist Carlos Oswald to have the statue's body act as a cross. And so, the design of Christ the Redeemer was finalized. The giant statue would have both of its arms extended as if it was embracing and welcoming people into Rio de Janeiro.

Christ the Redeemer alongside a set of antennas that inspired Heitor da Silva Costa.
Diego Torres Silvestre from Sao Paulo, Brazil, CC BY 2.0
<https://creativecommons.org/licenses/by/2.0>, via Wikimedia Commons:
https://commons.wikimedia.org/wiki/File:(2006)_Christ_the_Redeemer_(6955601775).jpg

Heitor might have played a crucial role in designing the overall look of the statue; however, the face of the sculpture was handled by Gheorghe Leonida, a talented and skilled artist who hailed from Romania. Leonida's task was to not only produce a sculpture with extreme precision but also capture the sense of warmth and spirituality of Christ in his work.

To breathe life into the Deco style of the statue, Heitor worked hand-in-hand with Paul Landowski, a French-Polish sculptor, who was put in charge of ensuring the overall aesthetic of the statue. Perhaps in his workshop in Paris, Landowski sculpted the statue's head and hands in their real measurement; sources claim the sculptor spent at least a few years perfecting a four-meter plaster model of the statue in his studio. Once completed, these clay sculptures were sent to Rio by boat. Only then would the craftsmen in Brazil work to reproduce the concrete models of the clay sculpture carved by Landowski—this process is said to have taken an extensive number of hours.

The statue's construction was still far from completion when Heitor was met with another challenge: the Brazilian engineer had to finalize the external finish of the statue. He was well aware that using concrete alone would not give the grand statue the astonishing finishing effect he had long envisioned. And so, he embarked on yet another quest to solve the problem.

Heitor soon got inspiration during his visit to a recently opened arcade in Champs-Elysees. Here, he was left fascinated by a Parisian fountain that had its walls lined with mosaics made of tiny, triangular tiles. With this fresh idea, Heitor experimented with various materials to determine the best choice for his grand statue. He eventually settled on soapstone, which was already commonly used in the many churches of Brazil. Soapstone was also popularly known for its resistance to fading, sun, and rain and withstand temperature fluctuations.

Later, the society women of the churches gathered to lend their hands to completing the meticulous structure. For hours, they worked together to stick the triangular pieces of soapstone to sheets of mesh, which would later be used to cover every part of the body of Christ—except the head and hands. Some said that the women would even write the names of their loved ones on the back of the triangular pieces before attaching the tile to the mesh sheets. This, they believed, would forever seal their love.

Without a doubt, constructing a gigantic monument on top of a mountain rising to a great height was not simple. In fact, many had wondered about the process of placing such a statue on the summit. Interestingly, the statue was not placed on the mountain all at once; instead, pieces of it were assembled on the mountaintop. Once they checked off all the materials needed for the construction—including the mesh sheets full of the triangular soapstone tiles—they transported these items to the construction site perched on the mountain. Special care was taken to ensure the safe transport of these delicate materials. A single crack in the concrete sculpture would definitely delay the construction work.

These materials were transported using a cogwheel train—the same one reserved for tourists who wish to explore the summit without climbing the steep paths. Water, on the other hand, was hauled from a fountain almost three hundred meters from the construction site. By scaling the scaffoldings, skilled workers would carefully lift and position the heavy pieces of the statues, which were installed with precise alignment and stability. Once the workers were done with the concrete structure, another team of craftsmen would use their precision skills to cover the entire statue with the triangular soapstone pieces. It is estimated that over six million pieces of tiny soapstone mosaic tiles were used.

The construction of Christ the Redeemer began in the middle of 1926 and took nine long years to complete. Unlike other colossal structures of ancient times, no lives were lost during the entire construction process despite all the significant challenges of working at such a great height.

On the 12th of October, 1931, the statue began receiving its first sets of visitors. A large gathering of tourists and locals, government representatives, and religious leaders gathered on top of Mount Corcovado to witness the inauguration of the grand statue. Towering over thirty meters tall—making it the third tallest statue of Christ in the world—the statue's outstretched arms span over twenty-eight meters. Combined with the panoramic views of Rio de Janeiro, the statue of Christ the Redeemer has become a famous landmark in Brazil, enthralling millions of tourists hailing from each continent.

The panoramic view of Christ the Redeemer atop Mount Corcovado.

Nevertheless, the statue was also not free from the clasp of disaster. Due to its location at the peak of a mountain, the majestic monument had to face the fury of mother nature. Over the years, the statue was forced to endure strong winds, heavy rainfall, and of course, terrifying lightning strikes. In fact, the statue has been struck by lightning several times during its existence. Fortunately, Brazil spared no expense to bring the statue back to its former glory. Despite the formidable natural obstacles, Christ the Redeemer remains on top of the mountain, posing as a symbol of unwavering faith and hopeful aspiration.

Chapter 9 - The Conquest of the Inca: Triumphs and Tragedies

Every man in the world craves power. Whether weak or strong, rich or poor, young or old—all have the ambition of having the world wrapped around their precious fingers. The same could be said for Francisco Pizarro, the Spanish conquistador, or conqueror, whose name rose to fame in 1532 upon his success at obliterating the Inca civilization. Unlike many powerful figures immortalized in history books today, Pizarro was not born with a silver spoon. He was, in fact, born into a rather humble family. Though his father served in the Spanish army as a colonel, his family was not wealthy, and his mother was described as the daughter of a mere farmer. Pizarro never had the chance to attend school, and he was believed to have grown up without knowing how to read or write.

Despite his unfair early years, Pizarro was always intrigued by tales of adventures in the New World. His urge to create a name of his own soon grew so strong that, in 1502, he left his home in Trujillo and embarked on a journey of fame and fortune. He first set sail to the Spanish colony of Hispaniola (modern-day Dominican Republic). Seven years later, Pizarro found himself in a failed expedition to the New World led by Alonso de Ojeda. It was only in 1513 that he began to take a step closer to the fortune he desired: Pizarro successfully rose as a captain under an expedition led by Vasco Nuñez de Balboa and became one of the first Europeans to set eyes on the Pacific Ocean. Panama soon became his home, where he obtained a successful political position and indulged in great wealth. Now a powerful mayor of Panama, it was high time for Pizarro to launch his own expedition and realize his dreams of having his name remembered by generations to come.

Obsessed with rumors of a thriving empire tucked in the obscure lands of South America, Pizarro worked to raise funds for his dream expedition. In 1524, he set sail to the northern coast of South America to confirm the rumors that had kept him awake most nights. However, it went south faster than he could gain information: many of his men were killed, while Pizarro suffered several wounds. A few years later, he launched another expedition against the wishes of the governor of Panama, who had begun losing faith in him. Nevertheless, his effort was fruitful this time. Pizarro and his men discovered the bustling town of Tumbes, which confirmed the rumors all along: a great civilization was blooming. And most importantly, they possessed an unthinkable amount of gold and silver.

To take on the mysterious natives right there and then would undoubtedly be suicide. And so, Pizarro packed his bags and returned to Spain, where he arranged a meeting with the king of Spain, Holy Roman Emperor Charles V. Supported by the newly discovered evidence, Pizarro presented the benefits of controlling Peru to the Spanish crown. Impressed, the king granted royal approval for the ambitious expedition. Pizarro was tasked with forming new colonies on the new lands and spreading Christianity. In return, Pizarro was made governor of all the lands he would be conquering and allowed to keep four-fifths of the wealth he would soon seize.

With the royal permission proudly in his hands, Pizarro returned to Trujillo and checked the first task off his list: enlisting reliable conquistadors to accompany his mission. His four paternal brothers, Juan, Francisco, Gonzalo, and Hernando, were among them. They boarded their ships in January 1540 en route to the Americas.

However, unbeknownst to the Spaniards, the Inca civilization was already battling a series of conflicts.

Several years before the arrival of the Spaniards, the empire was ruled by Huayna Capac, who gained the throne as the Sapa Inka (the monarch of the Inca Empire) in 1493. Although the Inca Empire was already at its height, largely thanks to his predecessor, Huayna Capac soon received daunting news that would mark the beginning of the empire's decline. Every day, the Sapan Inka received chasquis (Inca runners) who carried reports of the deaths of thousands in the north. They were believed to have succumbed to a mysterious disease that none of the Incas were familiar with. It arrived on the Inca lands a few years before Pizarro and his band of men could set their base for their conquest mission; the disease came from North and Central America.

Known to us today as smallpox, the Eurasian disease ravaged the Inca population as if there was no tomorrow. Sometime in 1528, those spared from the plague mourned the death of their Sapan Inka, Huayna Capac, who, along with his heir, was finally defeated by the merciless disease. With the deaths of millions, the sickness had unintentionally sided with Pizarro. Two years before he met with the Spanish king, the Inca had already lost nearly 90 percent of its population.

Left without a ruler, the Inca Empire was thrown into six years of turmoil as civil war erupted between the two remaining sons of Huayna Capac: Atahualpa and Huascar. While Huascar had his hands on most regions of the empire, Atahualpa gained support from his late father's veteran legions. And so, Atahualpa wasted no time leaving his seat in Quito and setting camp in Cajamarca. Bloodshed soon took over the empire as the civil war continued without rest. It finally ended in 1532 when Huascar's army was heavily defeated by Atahualpa's right outside Cuzco (the Incan capital). Huascar himself was captured, thus leaving the throne to Atahualpa.

Word of Huascar's defeat is said to have reached Atahualpa five days following the bloody battle—the chasquis delivered messages only by foot. Upon hearing the victory, Atahualpa again wasted no time planning his coronation. This, however, was not the only news he had received from the chasquis: the local chiefs had spotted 168 foreigners arriving on the shores of their land, with some riding "giant llamas." Atahualpa was also informed that these peculiar men were already en route to Cajamarca. Curious about the foreigners and their giant llamas—the Incas were not familiar with horses at the time—Atahualpa decided to meet them.

It is said that Pizarro and Atahualpa met twice. The first meeting was in mid-November 1532, and it was rather friendly. After all, the Sapan Inka was in a convivial mood following his victory in the civil war. Drinks were poured, speeches were exchanged, and the Incas got up close to the horses, a type of creature new to their realm. However, Pizarro never intended to maintain his friendly manner. The very next day, the

Spaniards planned to launch a surprise attack against the Incas under the disguise of a celebration. Pizarro had arrived in Peru a year before the end of the civil war and had been waiting for a golden opportunity to begin his conquest. Knowing Atahualpa had just ascended to the throne, the Spaniard invited the Sapan Inka to a feast to honor his victory. The supposed celebration was held at the main plaza of Cajamarca.

At that time, Atahualpa controlled over 80,000 men. Sensing no hostility, the Sapan Inka agreed to attend the feast. He brought 5,000 men, who were only armed with a single axe. Unbeknownst to them, Pizarro had carefully planned an ambush—the conquistador had hidden his heavily-armed men around the plaza. When Atahualpa arrived, he was greeted by the Dominican friar, Vicente de Valverde, who was also accompanied by a native translator.

The friar urged Atahualpa to accept Charles V as sovereign and to embrace Christianity. Sources claim that the friar went to the extent of threatening the Sapan Inka. The friar insisted that destruction was inevitable should the Sapan Inka refuse to convert to Christianity. Deaths following his stubbornness would also be entirely his fault. These words were a part of the Requerimiento, a document that proclaimed Spain's divine rights to conquests in the name of God. Perhaps feeling deceived, Atahualpa did the very thing Pizarro had hoped for: he angrily refused to fulfill the Spaniards' demands. And so, Pizarro signaled his men to emerge from their hiding and open fire, prompting the start of the famed Massacre of Cajamarca.

A depiction of the Massacre of Cajamarca.
https://commons.wikimedia.org/wiki/File:Inca-Spanish_confrontation.JPG

Trapped in the middle of the plaza with only narrow exits and armed with minimal weapons, the Inca warriors were easy prey to the Spaniards. Pizarro's small forces of 168 men shouted their battle cry "Santiago!" and, with their advanced weaponry, slaughtered the panicking Incas in just over an hour. All five thousand natives lay lifeless on the bloodied floor of the plaza, with only Atahualpa as the sole survivor—he was left unconscious following a blow on the head. Knowing the Sapan Inka possessed more value alive than dead, Pizarro held him hostage.

Atahualpa became aware of the Spaniards' greed; he witnessed how the Spaniards looted corpses and all the holy temples. And so, in exchange for his life, Atahualpa offered them a room full of unthinkable riches. The room was more than six meters long and five meters wide, and the captured Sapan Inka promised to stack it with gold and silver to a height of over two meters. The luxurious offer was undoubtedly accepted by Pizarro, though he never intended to fulfill his end of the bargain.

Despite remaining in Spanish captivity, Atahualpa never passed his throne to anyone else. Instead, he ruled his already crumbling empire from a distance, perhaps with chains around his wrists. Pizarro, on the other hand, was never known to have stayed still for long; he sent his men out on an exploratory expedition to Cuzco while he waited behind for reinforcement to arrive from Panama. Eight months passed, and as promised, Atahualpa had the room filled with the riches of the Inca. Today, the value of the treasures would be over fifty million USD.

An illustration of the Inca people bringing in the ransom for Atahualpa's release.
https://commons.wikimedia.org/wiki/File:Oro_y_plata_del_Inca.jpg

Probably thinking he could finally gain his freedom and quietly plan a retaliation, Atahualpa patiently waited for Pizarro's decision. However, the ransom was not enough to distract the Spaniards. In the eyes of Pizarro, Atahualpa had already exhausted his role; the Inca ruler had no other use to the Spaniards apart from posing a possible danger in the future. And so, on the 26th of July 1533, the once-mighty Inca king was sentenced to death by burning at the stake. Once again and for the last time, the Spaniards demanded that the hard-headed monarch accept Christianity. In return, should he agree, they offered him an easier way out. With his life already at the end of the line, Atahualpa agreed to be baptized. Because of this, Pizarro ordered the fire extinguished. He then granted—or condemned—Atahualpa to death by strangulation while his people watched, their eyes filled with terror.

A painting depicting Atahualpa's execution.
https://commons.wikimedia.org/wiki/File:Luis_Montero_-_The_Funerals_of_Inca_Atahualpa_-_Google_Art_Project.jpg

With the death of Atahualpa, the Inca spiraled straight into a dark abyss. Despite having fewer numbers than the kingless Inca warriors, the Spaniards—fully equipped from top to toe—easily trampled their way through Cuzco, sacking the entire city while plundering every fortune it hid. They then installed a puppet king named Manco to maintain peace in the empire. This move led to a rebellion three years later, but Manco and the Inca failed to reclaim their power. Seeing no other way, the Inca were forced to retreat to Vilcabamba, a village deep in the jungle. Here, they built their last stronghold. Perhaps protected and hidden by the thick greenery, Vilcabamba remained a safe haven for the Inca for about thirty-six years.

In 1572, when the throne had already passed to Manco's son, Túpac Amaru, the Spaniards finally took action. The last king of the Inca was executed without hesitation, closing the last chapter of the Inca Empire. Vilcabamba, on the other hand, was left under the care of mother nature. Though the Inca civilization was left forgotten following their terrible fate, the accidental discovery of Machu Picchu, a glorious mountain citadel, would soon revive the history of the Inca.

Chapter 10 - The Misidentification of Machu Picchu

Some say the once mighty empire of the Incas fell faster than the fleeting moments it had taken to rise and prosper. The Spaniards had moved swiftly to dismantle the Incan society with the help of great weapons and machinery while plundering all its riches and destroying its sacred sites. Their kings were executed as if they were nothing more than the lowest slaves, and their cities were razed until each was reduced to ashes or reclaimed by the forces of nature. Vilcabamba, for one, was swallowed whole by the relentless march of time, with encroaching nature hugging close to the many structures that once stood tall in the stronghold.

Even though centuries have passed since the fall of the ancient civilization, the legend of Vilcabamba as the famed Lost City of the Incas continued to intrigue the imaginations of explorers, historians, and archaeologists. Like the Spaniards, some even believe that the Lost City holds secret treasures left by the indigenous people. Those who do not have their eyes set on the vast riches of the lost civilization, however, are more captivated by the mystery of its history. Among those thirsty for the tales of the Inca was Hiram Bingham, a man whose curiosity and passion for South American studies invited him to embark on a set of extraordinary journeys of discovery.

Born in Hawaii, Hiram Bingham was neither a trained archaeologist nor an anthropologist but an obsessed explorer, academic, and historian. However, during a particular trip to Chile, where he served as a delegate to the First Pan-American Scientific Congress, Bingham first encountered remnants of the Incan ruins. Surprisingly, this was not enough to pique his interest in searching for the forgotten city of the Incas.

In 1908, Bingham found himself near Cuzco while working on an autobiography of the South American liberator, Simón Bolívar. Here, he was persuaded by a local to visit the site of the Incan citadel, Choquequirao. After a few moments of hesitation, Bingham followed the man to the site. As soon as the man pointed to the still-intact citadel, Bingham's curiosity level heightened.

Soon, Bingham returned from his eye-opening adventures and persuaded Yale University—where he held a lectureship position at that time—to collaborate with the Peruvian authorities on an expedition to search for more Inca sites in the Cuzco region. And so, in 1911, Bingham was made captain of the team as the expedition set forth, hoping they could not only find but unveil more forgotten cities of the Incas, especially the fabled Vilcabamba.

Bingham was confident he could find the city with extra hours of work. He spent his time studying existing documents, examining both old and new maps, and holding discussions with multiple experts and scholars to gain insights into the potential location of the forgotten Inca city. This was his daily routine until it was finally time for him to depart to the remote regions of Peru.

While the opinions and theories of the scholars were important and worth noting, Bingham also understood that the most precious information about the ancient ruins could be obtained from the local farmers and indigenous communities within the Peruvian landscape. So, he engaged with these communities, hoping they could provide guidance and new insights. He was, indeed, correct about listening to the locals. With their help, Bingham and his team navigated through the rough terrain with minimal obstacles and eventually laid eyes on more hidden remnants of the Inca. As he traversed through the Andes Mountains, Bingham talked to the local farmers. Fortunately for the curious explorer, the locals were delighted to share stories of the ruins and the supposed locations of the ancient sites. All the information led Bingham from one site to another. He studied each site and marveled at every structure he stumbled on. Bingham was indeed on the right track to revive the stories of the Inca.

While exploring the Urubamba Valley, Bingham's journey took a momentous turn. Here, he met a local farmer named Melchor Arteaga, who pointed the way to a mountainous jewel tucked away among the towering peaks. After hiking through narrow inclining paths and carefully avoiding slippery stones, Bingham finally arrived at the site. He was immediately greeted by dozens of perfectly carved stone structures, terraces cascading down the mountainside, and mysterious altars within the half-destroyed walls packed with stones of varying sizes. The enigmatic aura of the forgotten city undeniably captivated the explorer and left him completely awe-struck.

Photograph of Machu Picchu taken by Hiram Bingham III in 1912 after major clearing and before reconstruction work began.
https://commons.wikimedia.org/wiki/File:Machupicchu_hb10.jpg

Bingham felt elated; he realized he had stumbled on a hidden gem that had remained concealed for many centuries (though the locals were always aware of the city's existence). Remembering the descriptions he had come across, the explorer was fairly confident he had found what other explorers could not: he had discovered the fabled Lost City of Inca, Vilcabamba. The location of the ancient city, combined with the uniquely-built stone structures and the lack of previous exploration, further cemented his thoughts. However, despite his belief, Bingham was sadly mistaken. The city perched on the mountains was not Vilcabamba but, in fact, Machu Picchu, another Incan wonder that rarely appeared in ancient written records.

Machu Picchu, which in Quechuan means "Old Mountain," earned its name from the site's amazing location on the summit of Huayna Picchu. Standing at approximately 2,720 meters above sea level, one could feast their eyes on breathtaking panoramic views of the ancient city and the surrounding mountains.

One of many things about Machu Picchu that perplexes historians and scholars is its construction process. The Inca had no access to machinery and advanced technology, so how exactly did they construct such permanent structures that survived centuries? They did not use a single metal in their sturdy structures, and no signs of mortar could be seen holding the stones together. The Incas' absolute precision, combined with the intricacy of their construction, has raised many questions about how they successfully achieved such an incredible feat.

Archaeologists claim Machu Picchu was built over ninety years. Experts debate how the Incas transported the massive stones used in the many structures of the ancient city up the steep and towering mountain. Not only do the stones weigh several tons, but the Incas likely did not use any wheels to transport them from the quarries.

One suggestion explains that to achieve such a monumental task, the Incas presumably used a system of ramps and sledges to transport the stones. Using pure human labor and durable ropes, the Inca would have hauled the stones up the mountain. It could also be plausible that they benefited from the rainy season; on the wet and slippery slopes, they could have dragged the stones up the mountain without much friction.

However, another theory proposes that the Incas were masters of a technique called "stone rolling." Using round logs, they might have rolled the stones along them to move the construction material with as little friction as possible. This method is also believed to have been extremely useful for them to move larger stones and boulders.

The remains of Machu Picchu today.

No one can live long without water, and the Incas were, of course, well aware of that. To ensure their city could be properly inhabited despite its location almost reaching the skies, the Incas installed an extensive water supply system. Once they located the nearest water source—a spring on the north slope of Huayna Picchu—the Inca worked tirelessly to build a stone canal big enough to carry twenty-six gallons of water per minute in the direction of the city. At a location where the water would land, they constructed a stairway of fountains, which still functions today.

The entire city was constructed primarily using a technique the Incas were well-versed in. Known as "Idquo ashlar," this building technique could be seen in most cities of the Incan civilization. This method requires extremely high patience and precision; the Incas meticulously carved and shaped the stones in different sizes so that, when put together, the stones would interlock, ensuring a tight fit and stability. Even without mortar, the Incas could arrange the stones so precisely that not even a blade of grass could pass through them. The Incas had also taken account of the earthquakes that occasionally shook their grounds. The arrangement of the stones was so remarkable that they would move in rhythm with the earth's merciless motion. This allowed the structures to withstand the natural disaster with little damage.

The Incas might not have a written language—they recorded information using a system of knots—but they seemed to have had their own rules for designing structures in the city. The windows of the ruins, for instance, were typically the length of a forearm, while the space between them was two forearms.

Many more mysteries persist at Machu Picchu. The more research is conducted and extensive excavations are held, professionals gain not answers but more questions. The purpose of specific structures and the circumstances of the city's abandonment, for instance, remain unknown. It is safe to assume that Machu Picchu was built around the 15th century CE when the empire was at its utmost glory. But the purpose of the city remains a topic of debate, especially when Machu Picchu barely existed in written records—even its site was relatively unknown to the outside world until Hiram Bingham decided to hike the mountain paths.

At this time, we can only rely on theories proposed by numerous scholars and historians. Some believe that Machu Picchu once served as an agricultural and trading center since the city had vast agricultural terraces in the south (the north was turned into an urban center), and remnants of storage structures could also be found around the area. Its strategic location near the ancient trade routes also provides further support to this theory.

Terraces used for farming at Machu Picchu.

Seeing the ruins of intricate and fine living quarters and enough water supply, historians can also agree that Machu Picchu was a royal city or perhaps a place of retreat for the Incan nobility. Its hidden location and breathtaking views may have made it an ideal location for nobles to escape from the demands of ruling, governing, and protecting.

Another popular hypothesis proposes that Machu Picchu was an important religious site. The ancient city was also dotted with temples, ceremonial altars, and stone carvings possibly depicting religious symbols of a spiritual aspect. Some believe it was a place of pilgrimage, while others think it was a sacred dwelling for Incan priests and spiritual leaders.

One of the several religious buildings on the complex, the Temple of the Sun, has been recognized for holding great significance in the Incas' religious beliefs. In Incan mythology, Inti was referred to as the representation of the sun. Unsurprisingly, Inti claimed to have possessed mighty life-giving powers and was once revered as the most important deity. Since the sun was perceived as the main source of energy, warmth, and fertility, Inti played a big role in sustaining the agricultural abundance and prosperity of the Incan people. Abandoning the god could invoke his wrath; without their god's blessings, it would be impossible for them to live in peace and harmony.

The remnants of the Temple of the Sun.
https://commons.wikimedia.org/wiki/File:Machupicchu_intihuatana.JPG

As such, the Inca worshipped Inti fervently. They showcased their near-perfect skills in stonemasonry by constructing a temple in the middle of the city sacred to Inti. Within the temple, they placed a stone altar. Here, the priests held many rituals, ceremonies, and sacrificial offerings aimed to please the sun god and give him the honor he deserved for showering the Inca with bountiful harvests. However, these religious ceremonies were not done at random times. Scholars have proposed that the temple also served as an observatory.

Perhaps the most prominent feature of the temple is the trapezoidal windows, which perfectly frame views of the surrounding mountains and the sacred landscape—presumably connecting the temple with the celestial realm of the gods. Using these two windows, the Incan priests would observe the sky and track the movement of the sun to align their rituals with the celestial cycles. The two windows were perfectly positioned so that, during the winter or summer solstice, the sun's rays would shine through one of the windows and land on the stone altar. This was the perfect time for sacrifices and offerings.

The Temple of the Sun also has another intriguing feature. Located right beneath the temple is an underground cave or mysterious chamber that none were permitted to enter. Known as the Royal Tomb or the Royal Mausoleum, the chamber is believed to have been the eternal home to a deceased Incan king. Since the Incas deeply revered their ancestors, preserving their rulers' bodies was vital to their spiritual beliefs. Once mummified, the body was possibly taken to the chamber to be put to a proper rest—though not a single body has ever been retrieved from the cavern. Many suspect that the mummy of Pachacuti, the Incan king who commissioned the city's construction, has been resting among mountains of gold and silver behind the Secret Door of Machu Picchu. This mysterious sealed entrance, however, has been left untouched due to the restrictions imposed by the Cuzco Ministry of Culture.

Another temple can also be found on the back slope of Huayna Picchu. Known to us today as the Great Cavern, or the Temple of the Moon, this sacred site was carved out of a shallow cave. It boasted a few trapezoidal windows, which scholars suggest were used as lookout spots, and a set of fake doors. Caves were important to the Incas: they were considered the middle world between the living and the dead. Therefore, just like the Temple of the Sun, it is completely possible the temple once served as an important sacred site where ritualistic traditions and practices were performed.

The Temple of the Sun.

Nevertheless, the theories of the real function of Machu Picchu are not mutually exclusive, as the ancient city might have served multiple purposes simultaneously. After all, the Incas were widely known for their complex and layered societal structure, so the city could have been inhabited and used for various functions.

Hiram Bingham is said to have believed he had found the legendary Lost City of the Incas until his last breath. Though his quest for Vilcabamba may not have led him to the exact destination he sought—the real Lost City of the Inca was eventually discovered in 1964, eight years after Bingham's death—his effort to unveil the buried history of the lost civilization cannot be overlooked. Despite his misidentification, his unearthing of Machu Picchu successfully brought the ancient civilization to the world's attention. Today, Machu Picchu is an icon of human ingenuity, cultural heritage, and natural beauty.

Chapter 11 - Shah Jahan, the Rise of the Man Who Built the Taj Mahal

The Mughal Empire was one of the world's most powerful empires during the early modern period. The Mughal rulers established an empire that spanned much of the Indian subcontinent, parts of modern-day Afghanistan, and parts of modern-day Pakistan.

However, just like the rest of the world, the Mughal Empire was not at all free from the tight grasp of constant war and bloodshed. In 1605, the empire welcomed its new ruler, Jahangir, to the throne. His succession was not well-received by everyone, especially Khusrau Mirza, his own flesh and blood. Leveraging on his position as the favorite prince of the former emperor and grandfather, Akbar, Khusrau rallied his supporters and launched a rebellion against Jahangir to claim the throne.

Civil war ensued between the father and son, but it did not take long for Jahangir to emerge victorious. In 1606, Khusrau was captured and imprisoned in the fort of Agra (the empire's capital at the time) following his second failed rebellion. Unfortunately, peace was never meant to stay long within the Mughal Empire as another revolt broke out sixteen years later. This time, it was spearheaded by Jahangir's beloved son, Khurram.

Jahangir's third son, Khurram, did not enjoy a close relationship with his father in his early years. He was, instead, loved by his grandfather, the Great Akbar, who eventually took him under his wing. Predicting that his grandson would soon bring his empire to prosper, Akbar and his wife Ruqaiya raised the prince in their household, treating him equally as a beloved grandson and a royal prince. As a prince expected to take the reins when the time came, Khurram was supplied with endless education, from martial arts to languages and cultural arts such as literature, poetry, and music. It was only after Akbar's death that Khurram returned to the care of his mother, Jagat Gosain. Though separated at birth, the two shared a close bond; Khurram was engulfed in terrible sadness when Gosain died in 1619.

Khurram's relationship with Jahangir, on the other hand, was complex. Despite Jahangir's recognition of his son's military and administrative skills, he was, initially, rather distant. Khurram was sent on important diplomatic missions and entrusted with the leadership of various military campaigns, but he was not at all immune to the political tensions and conflicts that took place in the Mughal court. He spent most of his time enhancing his education and training and building his own network of supporters within the Mughal court–which would be useful when the time came.

Jahangir and Khurram's relationship began to shift when Khurram began relaying important information about his half-brother. He paid no mind to the father-son feud initially but soon realized there was an opportunity for him to shine if he participated in the matter. Over time, Jahangir began to favor Khurram and unofficially named him his heir-apparent, granting him full authority over Hisar-e-Feroza, a city traditionally given to the official heir-apparent of the Mughal Empire. This newfound favor put Khurram in a comfortable position within the imperial court, as he was constantly assured that he would be the one to take over the empire once Jahangir passed. However, this all changed when Nur Jahan, Jahangir's chief consort, devised a plot to disrupt Khurram's path to the throne.

Nur Jahan was never fond of Khurram and very much preferred her son-in-law, Shahryar Mirza, whom she thought could be easily manipulated, to gain the throne. And so, when Jahangir's health began to deteriorate due to his addiction to opium and wine, Nur Jahan took the golden opportunity to begin her plot. Although Jahangir was the one sitting on the throne, he could not oversee every state matter due to his declining health. And so, the real power behind the throne was Nur Jahan. To strengthen her power, she whispered words into her husband's ears so that her near relatives and supporters would gain

79

positions in the court.

She then sent Khurram on campaigns and missions far from the Mughal capital, hoping his reputation and influence in the court would cease. Without Khurram in court, Nur Jahan was able to carve ways for Shahryar to rise as a possible contender for the throne. However, Khurram eventually sensed his influence waning and discovered Nur Jahan's intentions. Almost immediately, the ambitious prince took matters into his own hands. He raised an army to march against his father for allowing Nur Jahan's plot to derail his chances of becoming an emperor.

And so, in 1622, Khurram led a rebellion, though it was nothing short of a failure. Just as when Khusrau attempted to show his teeth over a decade before, Jahangir defeated Khurram and dispersed the rebellion. In contrast to Khusrau, who was partially blinded and forced to watch his supporters slaughtered as a punishment (he was also later killed), Khurram was fully pardoned in 1626, though he completely lost favor with his father.

Jahangir, on the other hand, had been filling his time with travels due to the serious illness that had clung to him following his addiction. By 1627, the emperor departed to Kabul and Kashmir, hoping he could find a cure. Despite his effort to heal his sickness, his health unfortunately deteriorated. Beginning with a terrible cold, his addictions finally took a toll on what remained of his life; Jahangir passed away in the same year while traveling from Kashmir to Lahore. As he died far from home, his entrails were removed to preserve his body. He was temporarily buried in Baghsar Fort before being moved to Lahore and put to eternal rest in his own mausoleum in Shahdara Bagh. This is a location many believe held a special place in Jahangir's heart as it was a spot he frequented with his beloved wife, Nur Jahan.

The death of Jahangir undoubtedly caused another series of chaotic events to spread across the empire. The contenders for the imperial throne were actively engaged in a battle of succession. Khurram was left with no choice but to face his half-brother, Shahryar Mirza, who had managed to claim the throne with the support of Nur Jahan. Nevertheless, Shahryar only reigned for three short months as Khurram, with the help of Asaf Khan, his father-in-law, eventually emerged victorious in the feud. And so, Khurram finally realized his dream. At the beginning of 1628, Khurram was crowned the fifth emperor of the

Mughal Empire, changing his name to the one more familiar to us today: Shah Jahan.

The Mughal Empire saw a path to glory the very moment Shah Jahan took the reins. Perhaps rewarding his father-in-law for his loyalty, Shah Jahan gave Asaf Khan the position of vizier. Despite her failed quest for power, Nur Jahan was not killed but was forced to live the rest of her life under house arrest in Lahore. Shah Jahan is also believed to be a ruler who valued talent. A few years earlier, the emperor had met Mahabat Khan, who, under the strict order of Jahangir, had successfully put a stop to Shah Jahan's rebellion. Valuing his exceptional commanding skills, Shah Jahan chose to bury the past and made Mahabat Khan the governor of Ajmer.

While accepted by many of his subjects, like his predecessors, Shah Jahan could not escape from rebellions held by those who opposed his reign. Shortly after the coronation, the new emperor knew he must prepare to leave his seat in the capital upon receiving news of treachery from a certain Afghan nobleman. Khan Jahan Lodi, who had a close relationship with Jahangir, had gained great importance in the Mughal court. He was made the army's commander-in-chief by Jahangir following Shah Jahan's rebellion a few years previous and held the position of the governor of Deccan when Shah Jahan claimed the throne.

Khan Jahan Lodi had already soured his relationship with Shah Jahan after failing to express his support for the emperor's succession. However, Khan Jahan crossed the line when he allowed himself to be bribed by the Sultan of Ahmednagar. In return for money, Khan Jahan handed over lands entrusted to his governorship to the sultan. This was indeed treason in the eyes of the Mughal emperor.

And so, Shah Jahan laid out his plans to arrest the traitor by announcing a promotion for Khan Jahan. He must adhere to the Mughal protocol, which was to present himself before the emperor. However, Khan Jahan immediately sensed it was a clever trap, so he fled to Ahmednagar with his family. After obtaining support from the reigning sultan, Khan Jahan confidently marched toward Mughal territory, hoping he could start an invasion. This, of course, failed terribly. When news of Shah Jahan's advancement reached the sultan of Ahmednagar, he immediately withdrew his support for Khan Jahan; the sultan was terrified that Shah Jahan might lay an attack on his realm should he continue supporting the rebels.

Despite being left with only the support of various Afghan tribes, Khan Jahan remained resolute in his determination to challenge the Mughal army. Without hesitation, he and his supporters faced their opponents head-on in a fierce battle. The rebels were said to have fought valiantly, though their efforts were ultimately in vain. They were terribly defeated, and their leaders, including Khan Jahan and his son, were executed by decapitation. In a show of power, Shah Jahan displayed their severed heads at the gate of his palace, which acted as a grim warning to those who might consider defying his rule.

With the Mughal administration in a state of order and the threat of rebellion successfully dealt with, Shah Jahan turned his attention to restructuring the empire. He understood the importance of a strong military force to pursue his ambitions of expansion and, thus, began expanding his forces. By 1648, the Mughal Empire boasted over 900,000 well-trained infantry, artillerymen, and musketeers, with an additional 185,000 sowars (mounted soldiers), commanded by Mughal princes and nobles, forming a formidable cavalry unit.

Shah Jahan not only focused on military expansion but also issued several policies aimed at curbing the rising piracy and slavery in Bengal. Through a combination of military force, incentives, conciliation, and diplomacy, Shah Jahan brought renegade tribes under Mughal rule. Several years following his coronation, Shah Jahan brought his realm to its zenith. The Mughal Empire had riches many would envy, and his subjects lived their lives safe and sound most of the time.

Shah Jahan was a ruler who excelled not only in military strategy but also in promoting the arts and culture of the Mughal Empire. His grandfather Akbar might have laid the foundation for artistic expression in the empire, but Shah Jahan brought it to soaring new heights. Even before his ascent to the throne, Shah Jahan had initiated several impressive building projects throughout the Mughal territories, including the construction of mosques, gardens, and forts. However, after he assumed the crown, his creative vision truly flourished, with many of his commissions and constructions appearing even grander and more magnificent. To this day, Shah Jahan is considered one of the greatest patrons of Mughal architecture.

However, it was an event that took place in June 1631 that led to his grandest creation. Standing strong today, the magnificent structure is known as the Taj Mahal, and it was built out of Shah Jahan's undying love for his wife, Mumtaz Mahal.

Chapter 12 - The Taj Mahal: A Symbol of Love Beyond Measure

When the Mughal Empire was at its peak, Agra served as more than the political capital. In fact, it held an even greater significance. Its strategic location along the banks of the Yamuna River allowed the great city to transform and flourish into an economic hub, attracting an array of merchants, artisans, and traders from each corner of the world. Bazaars often became the bustling hub of commerce where traders and merchants found their best customers. At the time, it was common to see the busy marketplace fully adorned with diverse goods, each specially crafted with meticulous skill by experienced artisans and craftsmen.

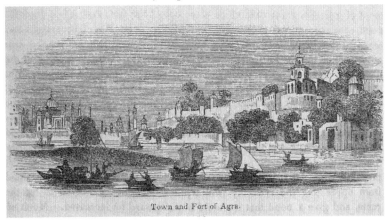

An illustration of the city of Agra.
https://commons.wikimedia.org/wiki/File:Town_and_port_at_agra.jpg

In these bazaars, a world of colors, scents, and sounds unfolded before the eyes of eager visitors. Stall after stall lined the narrow lanes, impressing passersby with their captivating displays. While shoppers were busy bantering with the merchants, hoping they could get the best deal, artisans showed off their craftsmanship by carving ornate designs on expensive wood. The air was filled with the exciting melodies of musicians playing all sorts of instruments.

However, shopping was not always why these bazaars were packed with visitors. Charity sales and fundraising events were occasionally held to support the less fortunate, provide relief during times of famine and natural disasters, or fund ambitious public infrastructure projects. Whenever these events were planned and announced, the nobles and wealthy businessmen would join hands to support the cause, either making substantial financial contributions or donating valuable items to be auctioned.

It is believed that Shah Jahan was present at one such charity sale when he was fifteen. It was not a typical event but one that would remain one of his core memories. Perhaps accompanied by his father, Jahangir, Shah Jahan strolled through the bazaar. While his father mingled with his subjects, whose hearts were eager to contribute to the noble cause, Shah Jahan was impressed by the vibrant sight of the colorful marketplace. His youthful eyes lit with curiosity as he wandered through the narrow yet beautifully adorned streets.

He visited one stall after the other, amazed by the crafts and textiles on the walls, each sporting a kaleidoscope of colors. It was only when his gaze fell on one particular individual that his feet froze. As he was standing by a stall selling beads and silk fabrics, Shah Jahan locked eyes with a girl whose presence, in his eyes, illuminated the entire bazaar—one gaze, and the future emperor had understood the true meaning of ethereal beauty. Though only a few words were exchanged, the two knew their hearts were connected and an enchanting bond was about to be formed. Shah Jahan might not have been able to spend much time wandering the bazaar, but he was glad to have at least learned the girl's name.

Arjumand Banu Begum was only fourteen when her radiance caught the attention of Shah Jahan. The daughter of Asaf Khan, a Persian noble who was also the brother of Nur Jahan (Jahangir's wife), it was no surprise her family held high regard in the Mughal court. Her best qualities—modesty and candor—were matched by her intellect and linguistic prowess. Not only limited to Arabic, Arjumand Banu was also exceptionally fluent in Persian, allowing her to hold meaningful conversations and compose heartfelt poems—a precious talent within the Mughal Empire. Although her great virtues made her an ideal match for the sons of many noble families, Shah Jahan held the only key to her heart. Shah Jahan had captured her heart entirely, just as much as she had stolen Shah Jahan's.

And so, when Shah Jahan expressed his love for Arjumand Banu to Jahangir, the emperor almost immediately agreed to have the two young lovebirds betrothed. However, their union would not happen until five years later. In 1612, Shah Jahan and Arjumand Banu were finally married. From then on, Arjumand Banu was bestowed with the title "Mumtaz Mahal," which in Persian means "beloved ornament of the palace." Indeed, as he became emperor, Shah Jahan had a few other wives, but it was only Mumtaz Mahal whom he held most dear to his heart—the rest were possibly married due to political reasons.

Mumtaz Mahal was a devoted spouse and an extraordinary companion who stood by Shah Jahan through thick and thin. Despite her pregnancies, she never failed to express her unwavering support and loyalty, accompanying Shah Jahan on his military campaigns and administrative tours throughout the Mughal Empire. Even during moments of political turmoil, Mumtaz Mahal was always present. She even stayed by her husband's side when Shah Jahan revolted against his father. Her presence in the Mughal court was indeed significant. She embraced the roles of a trusted counselor, advisor, and confidante to Shah Jahan.

Despite the immense love and adoration Shah Jahan had for Mumtaz Mahal, she never exploited her position to claim political power solely for her own benefit. Her focus remained on supporting her husband, nurturing their family, and contributing to the well-being of the empire. Mumtaz Mahal's humility and selflessness were remarkable, and she embodied the ideals of a devoted partner and compassionate leader. It is perhaps the embodiment of these qualities that intensified the depths of Shah Jahan's despair when tragic news reached his ears.

Even though he carried the burden of an emperor, Shah Jahan was not exempt from having his own dreams. Like many others, he wished to never witness the death of his companion. However, in 1631, as Shah

Jahan was on a military campaign in the Deccan Plateau, his nightmare began to turn into reality. Through messengers, the emperor was told of his wife's worsened condition: Mumtaz Mahal was about to give birth to their fourteenth child, but it seemed like she would not survive. Without hesitation, Shah Jahan rushed to be at the side of his wife. Perhaps while holding her hands, he prayed desperately that she would not die. But fate had other plans, as after nearly thirty hours of prolonged labor, Mumtaz Mahal passed away.

Some say the room went silent the moment Mumtaz Mahal breathed her last, while others claim it was filled with nothing but the emperor's wails of agony. We can never confirm his true reaction, but it is safe to assume that Mumtaz's death shattered Shah Jahan's heart into a million pieces. Ancient writers claim that his grief was so overwhelming that he fell into a deep hole of depression and mourning that lasted for years—or perhaps until the end of his life.

Humans do not have the power to meddle in matters of death; even the most powerful emperor of the Mughal Empire could not reverse the course of life and death. The most Shah Jahan could do was preserve the memory of his beloved wife. Even after death, Mumtaz Mahal deserved a grand gift for her unwavering devotion, love, and loyalty. And so, a magnificent vision took shape in the emperor's mind. Roughly seven months later, the emperor announced the construction of the Taj Mahal, a spectacular mausoleum befitting a beloved queen.

However, the Taj Mahal was not built merely as a tomb. As the patron of culture and architecture, Shah Jahan envisioned the marble structure going down in history as the world's most brilliant architectural masterpiece. And so, he gathered as many world-class architects as he could find; Ustad Ahmad Lahori was the one he was most confident could realize his vision. Not limiting the Taj to a single architectural design, Shah Jahan's team of architects concluded that to create a wonder, they must seamlessly fuse the diverse influences of Persian, Indian, and Islamic architecture into a singular, majestic structure.

The Taj Mahal.

Perhaps the most crucial step Shah Jahan oversaw before laying the foundation was the material selection. The Mughal emperor prioritized quality; hence, the architects and builders were only allowed to use the finest materials to build the magnificent mausoleum. These finest materials were sourced from the different parts of the empire and imported from lands beyond the frontiers. The white marble was brought into the empire from the city of Makrana in Rajasthan, India, while the jasper was collected from the Punjab region. Jade and sparkling crystals were sourced from China.

With the construction materials and precious gems gathered, the builders commenced their work on the Taj Mahal. On the southern bank of the Yamuna River, the first foundation of the wondrous mausoleum was carefully laid with extreme precision. Shah Jahan wished not to see a single defect in the grand mausoleum of his beloved wife. And so, it took over twenty years for the project to finally be completed, with an additional five years of constructing several other buildings and gardens at the complex.

The main gateway, Darwaza-i-Rauza.
*Matthew T Rader, https://matthewtrader.com, CC BY-SA 4.0
<https://creativecommons.org/licenses/by-sa/4.0>, via Wikimedia Commons:
https://commons.wikimedia.org/wiki/File:The_main_gateway_(darwaza)_to_the_Taj_Mahal.jpg*

The exterior of Taj Mahal and one of its minarets.
*Matthew T Rader, https://matthewtrader.com, CC BY-SA 4.0
<https://creativecommons.org/licenses/by-sa/4.0>, via Wikimedia Commons:
https://commons.wikimedia.org/wiki/File:Taj_Mahal_Exterior_with_a_minaret.jpg*

Shah Jahan was around fifty-six when the mausoleum marvelously stood before his eyes. As he took his first steps into the Darwaza-i-Rauza (the main gateway), he was immediately welcomed by the Taj's grandeur and expensive ornamentation. Adorned with uniquely designed geometric patterns and floral motifs, the gateway served as the grand entrance into the world of unparalleled beauty that lay beyond. Perhaps it was at this moment that Shah Jahan realized that his wish had eventually come true: the Taj Mahal was indeed perfect in his eyes.

Beyond the main gateway was a serene garden known as the Charbagh. The garden was divided into four symmetrical sections using water channels, which sources suggest represent the four flowing rivers of paradise in Islamic beliefs. However, the central focus of the complex is the mausoleum. One cannot help but become awe-stricken by the perfect proportions and graceful curvature of the dome crowning the marble structure sitting on its elegant squared platform. On each side of the Taj Mahal are two pairs of minarets rising about 137 feet. Interestingly, all four minarets were built with a peculiar angle: tilted slightly outwards. This was implemented as a safety measure in the event of earthquakes. Should the ground shake, the slender minarets would fall away from the main mausoleum, protecting it from potential damage.

Within the mausoleum itself was the cenotaph of Mumtaz Mahal, which had been precisely placed at the center axis of the chamber. Shah Jahan's cenotaph was added later and placed right by his wife's. Surprisingly, these two cenotaphs are actually empty. They serve only as false tombs. The remains of the two loving royals were put to rest in a sealed chamber on a lower level right underneath the false tombs.

The false tombs of Mumtaz Mahal and Shah Jahan.
Gary Todd from Xinzheng, China, CC0, via Wikimedia Commons:

The actual tombs of Mumtaz Mahal and Shah Jahan in the lower level of Taj Mahal.

Regardless of the false tombs, the chamber is, indeed, extraordinary. It was meticulously adorned with exquisite carvings and ornamentations—after all, the Taj Mahal is renowned for its decorative elements. The calligraphy of the Quranic inscriptions, for instance, has been revered by many as one of the finest and most intricate forms of art. Skilled artisans and calligraphers were hired to work hand-in-hand, carving verses from the Quran onto the marble surfaces. Using the pietra dura technique, the craftsmen would inlay perfectly cut and polished gems such as jasper and jade into the marble, creating exceptionally elaborate patterns and motifs alongside the calligraphy.

Nearly every part of the Taj Mahal is symmetrical—except one. Although considered the most intricate section of the complex, the tomb chamber of Mumtaz Mahal is the only part that breaks the symmetrical design of the mausoleum. Whether this was intentional remains debatable. Legend has it that Shah Jahan never intended to have his own remains buried within the same mausoleum as his wife. Instead, he planned to construct another mausoleum similar to the Taj Mahal except for its color: appearing black and built right across from the Taj Mahal, Shah Jahan's mausoleum would have mirrored and complemented that of his late wife's. This plan, however, was probably disrupted due to his unexpected death. And so, without his own mausoleum, Shah Jahan was buried right by his wife. His cenotaph was placed slightly west of the central axis of the mausoleum, thus disrupting the structure's entire symmetry.

Many might agree that another of the Taj Mahal's remarkable features is its ever-changing colors, which depend on the time of day. At either dawn or dusk, the mausoleum appears to have hues of pink and orange. When the marble structure is met with bright rays of sunlight, the Taj Mahal gleams with a radiant white brilliance, stealing the attention of passersby and even those on the opposite side of the Yamuna River. The mausoleum's ethereal beauty is further enhanced by the reflecting pool.

Shah Jahan achieved many triumphs in his life as the emperor of the Mughal Empire, but it was his architectural contributions that are often highlighted in history books and documentaries. Following the completion of the Taj Mahal, the emperor reigned for only eighteen more years. In 1657, Shah Jahan fell ill and was left bedridden. His worsened condition led to a struggle of succession among his own flesh and blood. Eventually, one of his sons, Aurangzeb, emerged victorious in the power struggle and seized the opportunity to claim the throne.

Although Shah Jahan ended up recovering from his sickness, his son deemed him incompetent. And so, Shah Jahan was deposed and subjected to house arrest in the Agra Fort. Here, he spent the remainder of his days in seclusion; he could marvel at his beloved creation, the Taj Mahal, only from a distance. He was finally reunited with his beloved wife in 1666.

The Mughal Empire was ushered into an era of architectural wonder when Shah Jahan first wore the mantle of an emperor. His death, however, marked the end of an era; none of the structures commissioned by his successor could stand close to the Taj Mahal.

Unlike many other wonders of the ancient and new world, the Taj Mahal was never abandoned. The mausoleum remained under the guardianship of the Mughal Empire, with subsequent emperors overseeing its preservation and maintenance. It survived through the rough tests of time and continues to be remembered as a symbol of beauty and cultural heritage today.

Chapter 13 - The Rediscovery of Chichén Itzá

Central America was once a region of vast jungle and dense vegetation that hid many secrets and mysteries buried centuries ago. Before the 19th century, only a few people could say they'd explored the area, and even fewer could claim they had ventured as far as the ancient ruins of the once-thriving Maya civilization. One of the first to embark on such an adventure was John Lloyd Stephens, an American writer, attorney, and diplomat whose interest in the ancient Mesoamericans grew through his reading of early works published by the German explorer and naturalist Alexander von Humboldt. And so, when Stephens was appointed by the US president as the ambassador to Central America in 1836, he took the opportunity to explore and uncover the mysteries of the long-forgotten civilization.

With his loyal companion, the English architect and artist Frederick Catherwood, whom Stephens had met three years back, Stephens journeyed to Central America. They first landed in British Honduras (modern-day Belize), where they first laid eyes on the remnants left by the Maya: within the dense jungle was a series of ancient ruins that left them in awe. Indeed, most parts of the buildings were reclaimed by mother nature, with vines and vegetation covering them, but the intricate carvings and architecture were still visible. This was the ruins of Copán, a once-thriving city of the Maya civilization. With a payment of fifty dollars, the adventurers are said to have gained the right to draw and map the structures, allowing Catherwood to work his magic.

Copán was not the only Maya ruin the adventurers visited. From Belize, the two made their way to Mexico and Guatemala, where they stopped by Quiriguá, another intriguing ancient city of the Maya. In 1840, a year after their departure from the United States, Stephens and Catherwood arrived at yet another of the ancient ruins, Palenque. They remained on the site for almost a month, mapping and producing accurate drawings of the structures there, especially the popular Temple of the Inscriptions.

Behind every success lies great challenge. Despite having rediscovered ancient ruins, Catherwood contracted malaria during their travels. However, this did not stop them from moving on. In June 1840, the two arrived on the Yucatan Peninsula, where they explored the Maya city of Uxmal. Due to Catherwood's health condition, the adventure was cut short. The two returned to New York in July 1840. The following year, they continued their expedition to Yucatan, where they discovered over forty more ancient ruins, including history's most fascinating city, Chichén Itzá.

A photograph of Chichén Itzá in 1859–1860.
https://commons.wikimedia.org/wiki/File:Fa%C3%A7ade_principale_du_palais_des_Nonnes.jpg

The adventurers' rediscovery of the Maya civilization marked a pivotal moment in the history of the Maya. In his book, *Incidents of Travel in Central America, Chiapas and Yucatan,* Stephens recorded his travel accounts, which almost immediately brought the ancient Maya civilization to the world's attention. The ruins they found, especially those at the wondrous Chichén Itzá, opened the door for historians and archaeologists to learn more about this mysterious civilization.

The origin of the Maya civilization is still somewhat shrouded in mystery; however, historians and archaeologists generally believe that the Maya arrived in the Yucatan Peninsula around 7000 BCE. It is plausible that the Maya were originally hunter-gatherers from South America who eventually gave up their nomadic lifestyle for permanent settlements. Initially, they relied heavily on agriculture, particularly the cultivation of maize, which became one of their staple foods. These people also mastered a unique method of processing maize known as nixtamalization, which involves soaking and cooking the dried corn in an alkaline solution. This process made their diet more nutritious and less toxic. Apart from maize, the Maya also cultivated other plants, including beans and squash, to further supplement their diet.

As they developed, the Maya began trading with the neighboring Olmec civilization, which significantly influence early Maya culture. Perhaps mirroring the Olmecs, the Maya focused on constructing cities while practicing various religious rituals that would soon intrigue the rest of the world even after their fall. The Maya were indeed exceptional builders and architects. Not only did they develop their very own water purification methods, but they were also able to create complex trade networks and irrigation systems comparable to those of the modern world, all without the help of machinery and advanced technology.

Over time, the Maya civilization also developed its own hieroglyphic writing system, which possibly originated from those of earlier Mesoamerican civilizations. Compared to the Olmecs, the Mayan writing system is more intricate and sophisticated, comprising a combination of pictographs and glyphs that allowed them to record and document their history and religious practices. Impressively, close to 75 percent of their surviving writings, typically carved onto buildings and artifacts, have been deciphered today. The ability to decode these complex hieroglyphs has no doubt given us deeper insight into the colorful life of this lost civilization.

It is worth noting that the ancient Maya were extraordinary observers of the sky. Combining their fascination with the cycle of time and their knowledge of astronomy and mathematics, the Maya invented multiple calendar systems—some of which were considered almost accurate by researchers. The civil calendar, known as the Haab', comprises 365 days, separated into eighteen months of twenty days and a month of five days. In addition to the Haab', the Maya also used the Tzolk'in, a 260-day calendar believed to have been related to the movements of the zenith sun and the growing cycle of corn. While the Haab' enabled the Maya to keep track of time and seasons, the Tzolk'in helped them make important decisions, such as when to plant crops or hold religious ceremonies.

Another calendar that is more popular than the others is known as the Long Count. Often misunderstood in modern times, this particular calendar was used to measure a longer period; it was based on the number of days that had passed since a specific starting point known as the "Creation Date." The Maya believed that the mythical date of the creation of the human world was August 11, 3114 BCE. However, this particular calendar reached its cycle on December 21, 2012, a date many misinterpreted as a doomsday prophecy. In truth, the Maya never claimed the end of the cycle to be the end of the world, as it simply marked the beginning of a new cycle, just as we start a new year on January 1st.

During the Classic period (200-900 CE), the Maya civilization flourished to its peak. Their exquisite architecture was on full display; grand structures such as towering pyramids and sumptuous palaces were common sights across their various cities. Although a shared society, the Maya were never a united empire. Instead, the Maya lived in a collection of city-states, each governed by local kings. While earlier evidence suggests they were a peaceful civilization that only saw battles once in a while, recent findings have turned that view completely; researchers are certain the Maya were far from a peaceful society. Their thirst for power and control over territories often led to bloody warfare among cities. Tikal, Calakmul, and Caracol were some of the most powerful Maya cities that often waged war against one another.

Although we cannot yet confirm whether the Maya had professional soldier classes like the Aztecs, we can be sure that the military was important in their civilization. Members of the highest ruling class were selected from either the military or spiritual leaders of the respective cities, and their capture during battles was a key element of military strategy; capturing prisoners was a priority during war, especially high-ranking ones. These prisoners were often subjected to ritual humiliation at the victorious city or, worse, sacrificed.

The Maya built many cities throughout the years, with some of the biggest ones being Palenque, Tikal, Copan, and Calakmul. But the one that stands out the most and has received the utmost attention from all over the globe today is Chichén Itzá.

Chichén Itzá was once a thriving city on the northern Yucatan Peninsula densely packed with various stone structures ranging from temples to residential dwellings and commercial buildings. Established possibly in the early fifth century CE, Chichén Itzá was renowned as a significant center of political and economic activity in Maya society.

Although what remains of the grand city today are just ruins in somber hues of grey—the natural color of the stone—Chichén Itzá is believed to have been one of the most vibrant cities in the Maya realm. Traces of colors on several of the structures showed that shades of red, green, and blue were among the most common paints used by the indigenous group. Every structure in Chichén Itzá was also linked by a network of paved roadways—an impressive feat of engineering at the time, considering many European cities did not yet have paved streets connecting their many points of interest.

El Castillo, also known as the Temple of Kukulkan, is undoubtedly one of the most iconic structures ever built in Chichén Itzá. Towering in the heart of the city, this step pyramid was constructed in honor of Kukulkan, one of the most prominent deities in Maya mythology. Often depicted as a feathered serpent, the ancient god was worshipped for different reasons. He was typically associated with fertility, wisdom, wind, and agriculture. Some even believe Kukulkan had contributed to the advancement of the Maya; he is said to have bestowed on them the knowledge of writing, mathematics, astronomy, and of course, architecture.

El Castillo, or the famous Temple of Kukulkan.
Alastair Rae from London, United Kingdom, CC BY-SA 2.0
<https://creativecommons.org/licenses/by-sa/2.0>, via Wikimedia Commons:
https://commons.wikimedia.org/wiki/File:Chichen_Itza_(3326547826).jpg

Perhaps thanks to Kukulkan, the Maya were able to construct such a wonder. The El Castillo had four sides, each featuring a stairway of ninety-two steps. Including the platform at the top, the temple had 365 steps, representing the number of days in a year.

Measuring at least thirty meters tall, the outer walls appeared intricate. They were fully adorned with carved reliefs depicting serpents, warriors, and dozens of mythological scenes. As some of the world's greatest astronomers, the Maya used their expertise in constructing the temple: the location of El Castillo was not chosen without reason. Due to its precise astronomical alignment, the temple had a special visual effect. During both the spring and autumn equinoxes, the play of shadow and light on the stairway created an illusion of a serpent slithering down the pyramid, resembling a mythological scene when Kukulkan descended from the heavens.

The descent of the serpent effect demonstrated at Kukulcán during the night show with artificial lighting.

To the east of El Castillo also stands another grand temple known as the Temple of the Warriors. Due to its striking similarities to a particular temple in Tula called Tlahuizcalpantecuhtli, scholars were able to conclude that the Maya had once experienced an invasion from the Toltecs, possibly built between 800 and 1500 CE. The grand three-level pyramid was also known to some as the Temple of the Thousand Columns due to its many carved columns depicting warriors.

The Temple of the Warriors.

Spanning over forty meters wide, the temple was possibly painted in vibrant colors—small traces of colors left on what remains of the facade further support this claim. At the top of the temple, the Maya installed a reclining statue of an obscure figure known as Chac Mool. On its stone stomach is a bowl, which was probably used to hold sacrificial offerings to the gods.

Detail of the Temple of the Warriors, showing a statue of Chac Mool.
Bjørn Christian Tørrissen, CC BY-SA 3.0 <https://creativecommons.org/licenses/by-sa/3.0>, via Wikimedia Commons: https://commons.wikimedia.org/wiki/File:Chichen-Itza-Chac-Mool-2010.jpg

On the northern part of Chichén Itzá was another structure responsible for unveiling the beliefs and ritual practices of the Maya. Known as the Great Ball Court, this grand structure was once used by Maya society for a game called pok-ta-pok. The game was not played merely for entertainment and sports but held religious and ritualistic significance. The game was thought to be a representation of hunting and the struggle between life and death.

Measuring approximately 168 meters long and 70 meters wide, the court featured a stone hoop vertically mounted about six meters high on a wall at the center. In teams of two or four, the players had to pass a rubber ball weighing up to four kilograms through the hoop to earn a point or end the game. However, they were not allowed to use their hands or feet to throw the ball; instead, players must only use their hips, elbows, or knees, making the game harder than it looks.

The Great Ball Court.

Scholars claim that the game was played as a form of sacrifice to the gods. Often, prisoners of war were the ones forced to play the game. The losing team would then face their ultimate fate: they would be sacrificed on the altar in the name of their gods. However, that was not always the case. Pok-ta-pok was also played as entertainment, with children and women joining at times.

Perhaps the most sacred site of the city was none other than the Sacred Cenote. Also called the Sacred Well, this natural sinkhole was more than just a source of water. Measuring about sixty meters in diameter with a plunging depth of approximately thirty-five meters, the cenote was often used by the locals in their religious ceremonies. The Maya claimed the cenote as a sacred site; it was a gateway to a realm inhabited by entities higher than humankind, such as powerful deities and spirits.

The Sacred Cenote.

To display their devotion to the gods, the Maya commonly cast valuable objects, including pottery and gold, into the cenote. These offerings were thought to have the ability to please the gods; in return, the Maya would be showered with blessings and rejoice.

Precious goods, however, were not the only offerings thrown into the cenote's depths. Archaeological excavations have found the remains of over 200 individuals at the sacred sinkhole, suggesting that the Maya also offered human sacrifices to the gods residing on the other end of the cenote. Most of the time, these human sacrifices were to ensure protection for their community.

However, only one man would survive the treacherous fall into the depths of the Sacred Well. This special individual would commune with the celestial beings within the cenote and return to the ground with prophecies of his own power. When this finally happened, the Maya of Chichén Itzá must be prepared. This event would mark the start of their decline and the beginning of a series of catastrophes that would soon engulf the Maya civilization.

Chapter 14 - The Collapse of the Maya Civilization and Its Wondrous Cities

The atmosphere had just turned grim. The vibrant sounds of the villagers talking to each other and the sights of them tending to their crops were replaced with something unimaginably darker. Wooden arrows flew in the air, several passing through the flesh of the unfortunate. The clashing sound of obsidian blades was getting louder, and poisonous darts were extracting the lives of those on the ground. Dwellings burned, and corpses dotted the ground as if the city was slowly transforming into a graveyard.

This was a period of decline for the Maya society of the southern lowlands—a period that would eventually give way for Chichén Itzá to rise as the central power of the civilization. Although the exact reasons behind the downfall of the Maya are shrouded in mystery, it is widely believed that warfare played a significant role.

The Maya were warriors, so it was not a surprise when they took wars and battles to a new level. Located in modern-day Guatemala, a powerful city-state called Tikal had been engaged in a fierce struggle with its main rival, the city of Calakmul; they waged war against each other in a series of battles for slightly over two centuries. The Tikal-Calakmul Wars were considered a significant turning point for the Maya civilization.

The Tikal-Calakmul Wars were only the beginning of an end. Following the war, the Maya began to witness a shift in the balance of power, eventually leading to the decline of several Maya cities, including Tikal. Although emerging as the victor of the centuries-long conflict, Tikal was swarmed with its own challenges. At the same time, warfare continued to plague the southern lowlands, gradually shaking the stability of the civilization. This was when the Maya stopped focusing on constructing grand palaces and temples within their cities. Instead, they used all the resources they'd gathered to construct defensive walls that could encircle their entire settlement. Other less important structures were sometimes dismantled to make way for fortifications; some cities cut walls through the middle of existing temples. Even tombs remained unfinished, delaying the souls of their deceased kings from reuniting with the gods.

Apart from continuous wars, scholars claim that additional factors contributed to the decline of the Maya classic period. One of them was the recurring droughts that had terribly plagued the region. Even though the Maya were ahead of their time with water management and the clever construction of cisterns, the prolonged droughts took a significant toll on their agricultural practices.

The Maya had always been deeply religious people. And so, when natural disasters continued tormenting them for a long time, they interpreted them as signs of their gods' wrath. These wrathful gods were to be pleased, and this responsibility fell to their divine kings: Maya rulers were expected to fulfill their gods' needs at all times. And so, when the kings failed to appease their gods and bring forth the rains necessary to grow their crops, the Maya chose to turn against their kings, with some even dreaming of putting a spear to their throats. The drought-induced hardship eventually led to rebellions. As a result, more blood was spilled, including that of the divine kings.

Perhaps not content with the drought causing havoc among the Maya, their ancient gods also brought a few environmental challenges on them. Many historians argue that the lands in which the Maya settled were naturally challenging. When their cities rapidly expanded, they would require more land to house their growing populations. Because of this, they would often resort to clearing forests, which, in turn, increased soil erosion and further disrupted the delicate ecological balance. Thus, combined with endless warfare and natural disasters, the Maya gradually descended toward their darkest time.

While the Maya of the southern lowlands were on the brink of collapse, the cities in the north were enjoying the opposite fate. At this point, Chichén Itzá and Uxmal had just begun to show their first signs of great power, and they were quick to seize the opportunity presented by the decline of their southern counterparts. As for the Maya in the south, their hopes of standing on their feet again were most certainly crushed. They could no longer see their future should they remain in their once-thriving cities. So, they had no choice but to abandon their homes and migrate to the north in search of a new life. Chichén Itzá was one of the cities that experienced the arrival of these Maya. From then on, Chichén Itzá grew tremendously and quickly became the new regional power. These migrating Maya who made Chichén Itzá their new home brought a collection of new influences, skills, traditions, and knowledge. They were one of the factors that fueled the growth and development of the ancient city. Before long, Chichén Itzá flourished as a hub of activity and a center of magnificent Maya architecture.

With the city now under the spotlight of power, the Maya saw a shift in their political structure. Ever since the collapse of the southern Maya cities, the traditional model of rule by kings was put to an end. Instead of divine kings, ruling councils were established at Chichén Itzá, allowing for a more collective approach to governance. The city also established itself as a dominant force in the trade economy of the Yucatan Peninsula. Chichén Itzá thrived as a center of trade and commerce, which rewarded it with grand wealth and riches.

But, of course, its power was never meant to last; the prosperity of Chichén Itzá would eventually wane. Perhaps mirroring its southern counterparts, the reasons behind its decline vary. According to one theory, internal strife erupted within the city due to its association with foreign influences. Chichén Itzá was home to dozens of architectural wonders. But some of them displayed peculiar similarities to those of the Toltecs, an influential civilization from central Mexico. Because of this, scholars propose that Chichén Itzá was, in fact, ruled by Toltec migrants—or invaders—who had assimilated into the Maya culture. The Toltecs were once popularly known for their impressive architectural techniques. Their most renowned architectural styles include columns, warrior motifs, and images of serpents, all of which were present in many of Chichén Itzá's structures. This theory, however, remains a topic of debate among historians and archaeologists. Some believe that, at some point, Chichén Itzá was invaded by the Toltecs, who later assumed the titles of rulers; others deny the claim. Considering this theory, it could be plausible that not all Maya were content with being ruled by foreign leaders.

Regardless, one particular man, known to the Maya as Hunac Ceel, is said to have played a crucial role in shaping the city's destiny. No one can confirm why exactly he dreamed of overthrowing Chichén Itzá. He is believed to have been captured following a foiled attack on the city and was condemned to be sacrificed by being thrown into the Sacred Cenote. Surprisingly, Hunac Ceel survived the murky waters of the cenote, which impressed the Maya of Chichén Itzá. His survival was indeed thought to have been an omen of something greater. Upon getting hoisted up, Hunac Ceel told the others of his journey to the celestial realm; he claimed that upon touching the waters of the cenote, he made contact with the gods. He told them about many prophecies and things that were yet to happen, including his rise to power. Completely enthralled by the tales and prophecies, the Maya appointed Hunac Ceel as their ruler, which gave way for him to lay the foundation of a new city called Mayapan.

A panorama of the Mayapan excavations.
SiMeCaIS, CC BY-SA 3.0 <https://creativecommons.org/licenses/by-sa/3.0>, via Wikimedia Commons: https://commons.wikimedia.org/wiki/File:Mayapan_Panorama.JPG

Hunac Ceel's brand new city, though an impressive sight in its own right, fell short of the architectural grandeur displayed in Chichén Itzá. Nevertheless, under the reign of Hunac Ceel, Mayapan eventually thrived and claimed the title of a new center of power. Hunac Ceel also gave birth to the Cocom dynasty, which ruled the Yucatan Peninsula during the post-classic period.

Although his power had been gradually increasing and his city beginning to flourish, Hunac Ceel still harbored mistrust towards the rulers of Chichén Itzá. The city was his rival at that time, and he must seek reasons to start a war.

And so, just as the gods had favored him, an opportunity to spark a conflict arose when the bride of Ah Ulil, the lord of the city Izamal, was kidnapped by Chac Xib Chac, the ruler of Chichén Itzá at the time. Without haste, Hunac Ceel seized the golden opportunity presented before him; in the name of Izamal, Hunac Ceel waged war against Chichén Itzá. In the ensuing effort, the Mayapan ruler emerged victorious. With the rulers of the city finally dealt with, Hunac Ceel established Mayapan as the sole power of the region. Those who survived were forced to abandon Chichén Itzá and relocate to Mayapan, contributing to its growing population and development. Mayapan continued to prosper as the main power of the Yucatan Peninsula for over two centuries before being decimated in 1441 CE.

Following Mayapan's decline, the Maya were yet again on the verge of collapse—especially when a new group of foreigners violently announced their arrival on their shores. Bartholomew Columbus was among the first Europeans to make contact with the Maya. Upon being sent by his brother, Christopher Columbus, in 1502 to explore the island of Guanaja, he came across an approaching canoe that appeared to carry a wealth of trade goods from the Yucatan Peninsula. Intrigued, Bartholomew did not waste a minute before seizing control of the canoe. On board, he discovered an array of cargo ranging from cotton textiles to ceramics, flint-studded war clubs, copper bells, and a large amount of cacao. The canoe was also transporting a small group of women and children, presumably en route to be sold as slaves. Not planning to return to his brother with only a simple report, Bartholomew looted the trading canoe. The Maya captain was also captured by the Europeans to serve as an interpreter. Although the canoe was allowed to continue its course, news of the attack reached those who often traveled along the Maya trade routes.

The Maya were not renowned for hospitality, especially towards foreign faces. And so, when the Maya stumbled upon several Europeans—who had just survived a shipwreck—drifting towards their coast in 1511, they paid no mind to their explanation and immediately took them as prisoners. Some were sacrificed in the name of the Maya gods, while those who attempted to flee were made slaves for life. One exception was made for the Spaniard named Gonzalo Guerrero, who, through a showcase of military prowess, had earned a place in the Maya military ranks. He eventually assimilated the beliefs and traditions of the Maya: Guerrero not only married a Maya woman but also converted to Maya polytheism. It is believed that Guerrero stayed loyal to the Maya until the end of his life; he was among the warriors who fought against the Spaniards who invaded the Maya.

The invasion campaign against the Maya in Guatemala was led primarily by Hernán Cortés and Pedro de Alvarado. Unlike their conquest of the Incan civilization, which took only forty years to realize, their invasion of the entire Maya society proved to be far more challenging; it was undeniably a long process that lasted nearly two centuries long. By the time of their arrival, the Maya cities were actively at war with each other while certain regions were already facing smallpox, which had greatly affected their population. Leveraging these opportunities, the conquistadors asserted their dominance.

Another Spanish conquistador, Francisco de Montejo, had also set out on his campaign in the Yucatan in 1527, but his troops were decimated by the fierce warriors. Despite his loss, the conquistador established a small fort at Xaman-Ha'. The Spaniards returned to the peninsula four years later with bigger reinforcements. Planning to take the Yucatan from the north, Montejo dispatched his son, Francisco Montejo the Younger, to seize Chichén Itzá in 1532. His objective was to establish a capital on the site. Though the Spaniards successfully made camp in Chichén Itzá—the city was almost undefended, as it served only as a pilgrimage site following its decline—the Maya surrounding the area soon grew hostile. They laid siege to the Spaniards, forcing them to retreat to the ruins of the city.

With no signs of reinforcements coming to help and depleting supplies, the Spaniards were forced to put up a fight. They were obliterated by the local warriors. And so, when night came, what was left of the troops began to leave their post, abandoning their recently established town in Chichén Itzá. They eventually left the Yucatan Peninsula in 1535 but would soon return with greater strategies to take on the vicious warriors.

It was only in 1542 that the Spaniards successfully established their first important political settlement. From here, the conquistadors went on to conquer the rest of the cities dotted along the peninsula. Though the Maya actively led resistance and revolts against the headstrong invaders, the Spanish eventually emerged victorious; the conquistadors successfully incorporated all the lands once belonging to the Maya into their empire by 1697.

The Spanish colonization brought about drastic changes to Maya society. The indigenous people were subjected to forced labor on their own ancestral lands, and their resources were exploited to the maximum. They were forced to dismiss their beliefs and embrace a religion they were unfamiliar with. Should they refuse, death and punishment were always the result.

The Spanish conquest seemed poised to extinguish the vibrant flame of the Maya civilization. Their once-great cities, including that of Chichén Itzá, might have gone through centuries of abandonment and decay. However, the resilience of the Maya culture and identity proved indomitable. They may have faced extreme oppression and defeat at the hands of the power-hungry Europeans. But even after years, their spirits refused to be silenced and forgotten. The rediscovery of Chichén Itzá and many other Maya cities following their neglect have brought them back to life. Perhaps against the wishes of the conquistadors, the Maya civilization has been put into the world's gaze. Today, the Maya legacy continues to shine brightly, illuminating the many continents of the world and captivating the hearts and minds of people from each corner of the globe.

Conclusion

Like detectives who require clues to solve their cases, historians rely heavily on evidence to embark on a journey to the past. The field of history is based on facts; it relies on the analysis and interpretation of evidence and remnants left by those before us. Without these clues, historical narratives would be nothing more than weak speculations and conjectures. With traces of the past gone from our sight, we can no longer construct a comprehensive understanding of our collective human story.

Hence, preserving the ruins that once belonged to the hundreds of generations before us plays a crucial role in the world of history. These sites could equip historians, archaeologists, and scholars with the necessary information to piece together the puzzle of bygone eras. The Seven Wonders of the World, which have been captivating the imagination of people throughout the centuries, are the main characters in this context. While these wondrous structures are often revered for their architectural grandeur and artistic brilliance, their stories often end in tragedy. More often than not, these magnificent structures never survived the cruel test of time. The ravages of human actions further eroded these wonders, leaving only stones and dust for us to discover centuries later or, in some cases, only references in ancient documents.

One such example is the Hanging Gardens of Babylon, an architectural masterpiece belonging to the list of the Seven Wonders of the Ancient World. Believed to have been built in the ancient city of Babylon, this wonder was thought to have the ability to impress everyone who passed by it. Its ascending series of tiered gardens, each filled with various species of trees, plants, and flowers, provided a grand spectacle for those close to the city. However, despite the descriptions of the gardens that have long been passed down from one generation to the next, no physical remains of the wonder have ever been discovered. This poses an obstacle for scholars to definitively confirm their existence. Without even the tiniest bit of remains as evidence, historians are left with more questions than answers. The non-existent remnants of the structure render the Hanging Gardens of Babylon an enigma; scholars are forced to rely strictly on ancient records to reconstruct its history.

The mysterious disappearance or destruction of the Hanging Gardens of Babylon highlights the importance of preserving the remnants of the past—be it those constructed in ancient times or those born into the New World. After all, these archaeological ruins and artifacts are among the few things that can connect us to our lost ancestors and shed light on their stories. These things provide valuable insights into their cultures, beliefs, technologies, and daily lives. By examining and studying these remains, archaeologists and historians can piece the puzzle of history, revealing the secrets and mysteries of the people before us.

Apart from their historical value, these wonders of the world hold other significance to our modern society. They serve as powerful educational tools, inspiring curiosity and awe in people regardless of age. They provide tangible examples of human ingenuity and creativity, fostering a sense of wonder and appreciation for our shared cultural heritage. Simply put, the wonders can act as a classroom or even a laboratory for individuals young and old to learn and explore their potential. The preservation of the wonders can also bring many benefits in terms of economics. These sites attract millions of visitors from all over the world, which eventually contribute to local economies. Through these sites, cultural exchange will also be made easier. Visitors of all ethnicities, races, and religions will learn to appreciate each other's cultures, giving way to a more interconnected and tolerant global society.

While it may be too late to save the wonders of the ancient world—except for the Great Pyramids of Giza—there is still ample time to ensure that the wonders of the new world endure the passage of time. The lessons learned from the disappearance and loss of the ancient wonders serve as a constant reminder of the importance of proactive preservation efforts for future generations.

Preserving the wonders of the new world goes beyond mere nostalgia or admiration for their exquisite facades. These monumental structures are evidence of human progress, technological advancements, and cultural diversity. Back then, preserving the ancient wonders may have been a daunting task, especially when wars often resulted in the structures' permanent damage. However, in the modern world, we have the advantage of advanced technology and an improved understanding of the value of cultural heritage. The responsibility of safeguarding these architectural treasures is without question put on our shoulders. By actively preserving these sites, we can ensure that future historians and generations have tangible evidence of our achievements and aspirations.

Here's another book by Captivating History that you might like

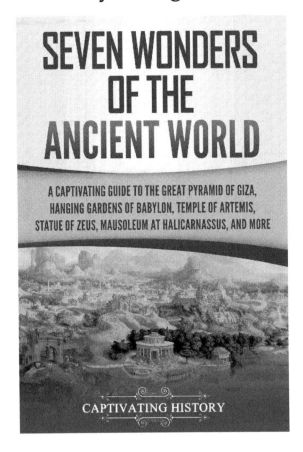

SEVEN WONDERS OF THE ANCIENT WORLD

A CAPTIVATING GUIDE TO THE GREAT PYRAMID OF GIZA, HANGING GARDENS OF BABYLON, TEMPLE OF ARTEMIS, STATUE OF ZEUS, MAUSOLEUM AT HALICARNASSUS, AND MORE

CAPTIVATING HISTORY

Free Bonus from Captivating History (Available for a Limited time)

Hi History Lovers!

Now you have a chance to join our exclusive history list so you can get your first history ebook for free as well as discounts and a potential to get more history books for free! Simply visit the link below to join.

Captivatinghistory.com/ebook

Also, make sure to follow us on Facebook, Twitter and Youtube by searching for Captivating History.

Bibliography

Bileta, V. (2021). Roman Theatre and Amphitheatre: Spectacle in the Roman World. TheCollector. https://www.thecollector.com/roman-theatre-amphitheatre-in-ancient-rome/

Briney, A. (2020). A Brief History of the Age of Exploration. ThoughtCo. https://www.thoughtco.com/age-of-exploration-1435006

Cartwright, M. (2023). Chichen Itza. World History Encyclopedia. https://www.worldhistory.org/Chichen_Itza/#:~:text=Chichen%20Itza%20fell%20into%20a,Mayap%C3%A1n%20became%20the%20new%20capital.

Cheng, L. (2017, February 14). Eight Secrets of the Taj Mahal. Smithsonian Magazine. https://www.smithsonianmag.com/travel/eight-secrets-taj-mahal-180962168/

Cottier, C. (2021). How the Inca Built Machu Picchu. Discover Magazine. https://www.discovermagazine.com/planet-earth/how-the-inca-built-machu-picchu

Del Campo, E. F. (2022, February 10). A husband's love built the Taj Mahal—but cost him an empire. National Geographic. https://www.nationalgeographic.co.uk/history-and-civilisation/2022/02/a-husbands-love-built-the-taj-mahal-but-cost-him-an-empire

Finelli, S. (2022). The Flooding of the Colosseum: Guide to Colosseum Naval Battles. The Roman Guy. https://theromanguy.com/italy-travel-blog/rome/colosseum/colosseum-naval-battles/

Great Wall Story - Meng Jiangnu. (n.d.). Top China Travel. https://www.topchinatravel.com/great-wall-of-china/meng-jiangnus-story.htm

Hardy, J. (2023). Inti: The Sun God of the Inca | History Cooperative. History Cooperative. https://historycooperative.org/inti/

Hunac Ceel. (2021). MayaIncaAztec.com.
https://www.mayaincaaztec.com/kings-and-emperors/hunac-ceel

Jarus, O. (2013). Spartacus: History of Gladiator Revolt Leader.
livescience.com. https://www.livescience.com/39730-spartacus.html

Khan, S. (2023). Changing Colours of Taj Mahal. Agra Taj City Tour.
https://agratajcitytour.com/changing-colours-of-taj-mahal-different-shades-and-colour-of-taj-mahal/

Mark, J. J. (2023). Kingdom of Nabatea. World History Encyclopedia.
https://www.worldhistory.org/Kingdom_of_Nabatea/

Riley, L. (n.d.). Christ The Redeemer. Seven Sisters Series.
https://lucindariley.co.uk/seven-sisters-series/the-seven-sisters/christ-the-redeemer/

Roller, S. (n.d.). Petra. History Hit. https://www.historyhit.com/locations/petra/

The discovery of Machu Picchu. (n.d.). History Today.
https://www.historytoday.com/archive/months-past/discovery-machu-picchu

Treaty of Tordesillas. (n.d.). National Geography.
https://education.nationalgeographic.org/resource/treaty-tordesillas/

Whitman, M. (2022). Hiram Bingham - Discovering Machu Picchu (Complete Story). Mountain IQ. https://www.machupicchutrek.net/hiram-bingham-machu-picchu/

Wikipedia contributors. (2023). Maya–Toltec controversy at Chichen Itza.
Wikipedia.
https://en.wikipedia.org/wiki/Maya%E2%80%93Toltec_controversy_at_Chichen_Itza#Modern_day_theories

Wikipedia contributors. (2023). Christ the Redeemer (statue). Wikipedia.
https://en.wikipedia.org/wiki/Christ_the_Redeemer_(statue)

Wikipedia contributors. (2023). Chichen Itza. Wikipedia.
https://en.wikipedia.org/wiki/Chichen_Itza

Wikipedia contributors. (2023). Ustad Ahmad Lahori. Wikipedia.
https://en.wikipedia.org/wiki/Ustad_Ahmad_Lahori

Printed in Great Britain
by Amazon

28605825R10073